ral Nappies Mess

it Wild D0278766 ed

ong Girl power Poo

Pubes Motherhood

Craptabulous Bang

ng Friendship Effin'

Sisterhood Chaos

oons Wine Saggy tits

t Puke Housework

Exhausion Bogeys

mpoo Periods Piles

s Imperfection Sex

Knee Deep in Life

Knee Deep in Life

Laura Belbin

EBURY
PRESS

3 5 7 9 10 8 6 4 2

Ebury Press, an imprint of Ebury Publishing
20 Vauxhall Bridge Road
London SW1V 2SA

Ebury Press is part of the Penguin Random House group
of companies whose addresses can be found at
global.penguinrandomhouse.com

Copyright © Laura Belbin 2020

Laura Belbin has asserted her right to be identified as
the author of this Work in accordance with the
Copyright, Designs and Patents Act 1988

First published by Ebury Press in 2020

www.penguin.co.uk

A CIP catalogue record for this book is available from
the British Library

ISBN 9781529107043

Typeset in 11/17.8 pt ITC Caslon 224 Std
by Integra Software Services Pvt. Ltd, Pondicherry

Printed and bound in Great Britain by Clays Ltd, Elcograf S.p.A.

Penguin Random House is committed to a
sustainable future for our business, our readers
and our planet. This book is made from Forest
Stewardship Council® certified paper.

To my three boys, Steve, Elliott and Toby, and my sister, Emma

Contents

You fucking got this

> *'I know you thought life would be all bleached arseholes, rainbows and screaming orgasms, and right now you're sat here reading this book with a nasty case of piles and a left tit that sags slightly more than the right.'*

Hello, my darling, *how are you*? I imagine it's been a while since someone asked you that? I don't mean that awkward-conversation-starter-on-a-first date 'how are you?'; I mean a you-look-like-you-could-do-with-a-hug-a-large-glass-of-wine-and-a-gentle-reassuring-slap-on-the-arse 'How Are You?'

We get so caught up with life sometimes that we forget to stop and congratulate ourselves for still being here. For somehow surviving this shitstorm and not killing anyone. It's a massive achievement. Pat yourself on the back. You did it. You're doing it. You.Are.Fucking.Awesome!

I know you thought life would be all bleached arse-holes, rainbows and screaming orgasms, and right now you're sat here reading this book with a nasty case of piles, a left tit that sags slightly more than the right, and the only orgasm you'll reach (after you've told your husband you haven't had a shit in four days, just because he touched your shoulder and you want to make it clear tonight's not gonna happen) is when you find that tub of Ben & Jerry's at the bottom of the freezer. You are tired. You are yet to see the bottom of the washing pile; it smells like old penis, and you keep toying with the idea of a cleaner, but you worry too much about The Judgement; after all, you've just found an old shit skid mark on the bathroom sink and you literally have no idea how long it's been there.

Basically, life isn't going to plan.

But I hear you. That person I just described? It's me. We all are *a bit*. It's just no one is saying it out loud because we are petrified of having it confirmed. Well, babe, if you're the skank then so am I. The woman with the shit-skid sink? Me. Often! I can't even tell you which house-dwelling human thinks it is appropriate to wipe their finger on the bathroom sink. My hope is that it isn't me but I can't be 100 per cent sure (*exhaustion is a bitch*).

I know you're wondering when the fuck it turns less *The Hills Have Eyes* and more *The Sound of Music*. But

I'm going to break this to you now: *The Sound of Music* is a crock of shit. Sorry, Julie.

We have this expectation as women that we'll keep a pristine house, raise model children and still find time to suck like a hoover, while mopping the floor with a broom shoved up our arse. It kind of grips my shit. Mainly because *it isn't really reality*.

This whole time you've probably been wondering how you're getting it wrong, without realising you've already been nailing it every single day. How? Simply because you get that beautiful ass out of bed each day and you never give up! (*By the way, I will reference that fine piece of ass on multiple occasions, so please get used to it!*) I get that you're probably thinking that's ridiculous, because you have no choice. And yet, babes, you do. You do have the choice to stop trying to change, give up and never bother to improve what you have. I want you to know you have FUCKING got this. You have this in a way I can't even describe because the people around you are happy because you are breathing; they are successful because of your support and they know they can carry on quite simply because you are in their lives. So, when is it your time to believe you are good enough the way you are? Yesterday. Which means you are absolutely overdue this little pow-wow.

> *'The truth is that the person you are right now has to learn to love herself, because that person beneath all the skin and chocolate gooey layers is going to be with you until you take your last breath. She needs your love and guidance; she deserves your support and kindness – not tomorrow, not when you have the perfect abs – now.'*

We always tell ourselves we'll be happier when we lose four stone and can see our hairy minge, because the roll of fat will have transformed into perfect abs, which you'll show off in tiny denim shorts in the playground as you collect the kids, and all the other mums will look on in utter disbelief because you've lost *So Much Weight*. I mean, wow, now you look like Sexy Susie Six Pack. But why does the four-stone-lighter version of you get all the fun? How come she gets to love herself and feel like she's arrived in life? No offence, Susie, babes, because, although I believe you are smoking hot with an ass I could bounce a coin off, you're not the person who is going to make you happy.

The truth is that the person you are right now has to learn to love herself, because the person beneath all the skin and chocolate gooey layers (if humans were made of chocolate, I would be serving life for cannibalism by now) is going to be with you until you take your last breath. She needs your love and guidance; she deserves your support and kindness – not tomorrow, not when you have the perfect abs – now.

We all believe that thin girls don't have hang-ups, that rich ones never have any worries and that girls who have cosmetic surgery bang their boyfriends nightly. But you don't need to be Porno Patricia to have a high sex drive. I know of women who live in six-bedroom mansions who have been at the food bank with next to nothing left to live off. And the thin girl? She's battled anxiety for most of her life. So remind yourself again who is nailing it best (and it's not always the cosmetic surgery hunnis nailing their husbands). All of us are nailing it, even through the shitstorm. No one is getting out of here alive, yet in the process – as we're all too busy smiling, disguising the truth – we forget that every single person has a story to tell and a heartache to share.

My mission, when I started blogging back in 2016, was to remind people they aren't alone, and that they are important to those around them. That can be lost at times when you're too busy trying to wipe your arse in peace, or praying for bedtime because the kids are doing your head in. So we continue to drag ourselves through life, not realising what a bunch of legends we are. This isn't about trying to be better than the next person, it's just about believing in yourself enough to know you can make a difference in your own life, and others' lives too.

No one likes a Sally Two Shits! Old Sally will always manage to trump the T-shirt you wear so proudly because the smug bitch will always have one more than you. I see so many people who feel the urge to compete

– it has become exhausting. I'd much rather stand in the corner of the room with a large bar of Galaxy and a double gin and tonic.

-Laura's Life Lesson- - - - -

Be less like Sally and more like Compassionate Carol, who high-fives the skid marks (not literally – that would be a shitmess) and celebrates the fact we all shit, piss and fart – who cares in what order – and there is absolutely no need to be bragging about it.

I can't say I've always been this laid back. I haven't! I shit you not, I didn't allow my three best friends around my house for over a year because I felt ashamed of how it looked.

I mean, there was a hole in the kitchen floor that you had to make sure you didn't stand on otherwise it would collapse. What The Fuck, Laura? Who even leaves shit like that for so long? And, yet, there I was, living in a house where you had to know where to step out of fear of losing a foot through the fucking floorboards!

I have come to the conclusion, after years of twisting my tits over not having the home everyone else has, that it doesn't fucking matter. The right people won't give a fuck about what the house looks like. I'd rather be part of a sisterhood busy empowering each other than talking about how they haven't put their washing away from last week.

I'm not sure when things changed for me. But I know that when I started blogging, I started seeing other women telling me they felt the same and that my blogs made them feel less alone. This in turn made me feel included. I was finally brave enough to say: look – this is me ... who wants to be part of my gang?! And people did! In fact, they already were.

I'm writing this book because I'm tired of seeing the lives we think we're meant to be living through the rose-tinted glass of social media, or in playground circles, where the mums pit their kids against each other in the hope they get to gloat about who did it better. I don't much like those spaces. Instead, a community of like-minded women have come together on Knee Deep In Life who support each other, even though they've never met. They laugh at the filth, they swear when things feel hopeless, they nod together in sadness and they celebrate not always getting it right.

I am always so emotionally overcome when I see women bravely sharing their story, sometimes about abuse, or being fat shamed, maybe showing their body in a bikini, and they are always met with hundreds of women replying, giving them support and encouragement. These women, this army of supporters, they are my kind of people and I am so proud to be a part of that.

I want to tell you more about how I got here, and – as I've always promised – I'm going to bring my good, bad and ugly, because we can't have the good without the ugly or the bad. Like anything in life, no matter how hard you work at something it'll never be perfect, and that goes for my own self-belief. I doubt myself often; there are days when my anxiety hits such peaks that all I can hear is the heavy beat of my own heart in my eardrums and the tight pain of crippling anxiety across my chest. We all need to remember that those moments suck, but they're there to make the good moments fucking awesome. I've learnt to breathe through these times, knowing they will pass, instead of believing they're here to stay for ever.

I want to ride this beast of a book into the hands of all of those people who doubt themselves, and my only hope is that it brings you the confidence and self-worth you truly deserve.

Have kids, they said; it'll be fun.
They said. I'm eight years in, with
a heavy dependency on gin, an
extra-large vagina and I'm 965
days overdue a lie-in.

1

Are we ready?

I guess this means it's time to be parents ...

> 'Our kids sometimes eat shit, which also includes sweets and biscuits, if it means they'll leave us alone long enough to allow us to sit and not be asked to do something. Fact.'

This job – parenting – it's thankless. It's exhausting, mind-numbing and a total fucking ball-ache. Right now,

I'm sat in front of the TV watching the same episode of *Bing*. You know the one – it's where he pushes the elephant off the swing. It's about to send me over the edge. *(Please, Flop, will you stop being a wet vagina and sort that kid out because he is irritating as fuck.)* And, I want to scream, 'I HAVE NO FUCKING IDEA WHAT I'M MEANT TO BE DOING!' Instead, I say those words silently to myself; they've become my daily mantra since … well, since the day I pushed my first baby out, to be precise.

I learnt pretty quickly that kids do not come with instruction manuals. My husband, Steve, and I have spent a large proportion of parenthood praying we're mature enough to keep them alive. I mean, we can barely manage ourselves (*takeaway number five this week, anyone?*). But thank fuck I don't do this alone because in all honesty having kids is fucking hard work. At the end of the day I take great pleasure in seeing Steve arrive home from a long day at work. I usually greet him with the 'hello' he always hopes for: 'I need a shit. They've been arseholes. I want to be left alone for fifteen minutes.'

Before we had children I remember I would judge women who didn't make food from scratch for their kids, who chose not to take them to groups where they knew no one. I would think it was sad they didn't do crafts with their kids. I now realise the bigger picture, which is that life as a parent is hard. Like, not just, 'shit, that was a rough day'; I mean, 'holy Moses, how can this many people need me all at once and why are they so loud??'

I was a bit of an arrogant idiot for thinking life as a parent was summed up in the perfectly filtered photos we see posted on social media. Those photos made it all look easy; the kids were smiling, and they looked like one massive happy family. But those posts appear and lead us all to believe it's just a walk in the fucking park, ending with a little embracing hug and an 'I love you' from your child. Even if that was the case (which it's not), you know they would have snot dripping from their nose and they would only be leaning in to whisper that they need a poo. These filtered photos lull us into the false sense of security that it will all just be alright, because no bastard wants to see little Johnny throwing a shit fit in the middle of Legoland when you've spent £900 to get in and four hours in the car telling them to calm the fuck down. I didn't expect us to be the parents whose kids cheer when we drive past a McDonald's because they make automatic assumptions that they are going in for food. I wouldn't mind but it gets embarrassing when it's 8.30am on a school day.

How can I bear to admit that? Because it is the truth, and why lie about it. I don't have the energy for pretending that our lives are any more glamorous than that. Our kids sometimes eat shit, which also includes sweets and biscuits, if it means they'll leave us alone long enough to allow us to sit and not be asked to do something. Fact.

*

Parenting came to me and Steve at a fairly late point in our relationship – we'd been together nine years. That was through choice, mainly because we were selfish pricks who liked to lie in and go on holiday. I was only 17 when I met Steve at his brother's birthday party. I bragged to my friends about how I was totally dating an older guy – a whole 18 months older. Truth was, we were still babies ourselves.

I'm so thankful we didn't have children then. It would have more than likely been the end of us because I now realise the pressure children put on a relationship. I always told Steve I needed to be married before I had children, not because I was religious in any way (*safe to say we had seen the inside of each other's anal cavities by the time we said 'I do' – I didn't wear white on my wedding day*), but because I wanted to make sure I had a honeymoon without children there (*remember the selfish prick remark. Yeah, that explains this statement well*).

I was desperate to be married; looking back, I have no idea why. We had a mortgage, good jobs, cars, the fucking lot, and all I wanted was a RING!!! A fucking RING, because nothing says you ain't getting rid of me that easily like a marriage certificate. And yet, when the day came for him to propose, I acted like a deranged beast from the deep. In short, I lost my shit!

I'll set the scene:

It's Christmas Eve (you'll realise in Chapter 7 that Christmas doesn't seem to bring us much luck) and

Steve has gone to work. There's a knock at the door; it's my parents' neighbour (he's such a close part of our family I call him my uncle and his wife was the witness at our wedding). Holding a rose. And a letter. Fuck!! It's finally happening!! After almost six years of waiting: the mortgage, the career, the car ... the RING!! I'm told to go to a local hotel, one where we had spent many an anniversary.

So, as I scream into the car park, having changed into my knee-high black leather boots, freshly brushed teeth and a quick once-over with a flannel between my fanny lips, I am READY!! I breeze into the hotel with an air of 'Fuck yes, I am moments away from becoming someone's fiancée'. I try my best to act casual while desperately trying to find my one true love, and I hear someone say, 'Hey, are you Laura??' My moment, it's so close! 'Yes, that's me,' I say, as I realise the woman calling my name is holding an arrow (*what the fuck?*).

'I've been told to give you this and buy you a drink.'

Well, this isn't funny! Where the fuck is Steve?? So, I chug the drink as quickly as I possibly can while holding an arrow (full-blown 'Robin Hood and his Merry Men will stab you in the face' kind of arrow) and feeling like the biggest dickhead. Around two minutes, four seconds later, I go to leave, and she says, 'You need to open the scroll around the arrow for your next clue.'

I'm already pretty pissed off; it's Christmas Eve and my house looks like the devil's arsehole and I'm not in the fucking mood. Next place, my nan's nursing home. Nothing like being greeted with a wall of piss smell as you walk into a building, is there?! Dressed like Julia Roberts in *Pretty Woman* (and I'm talking about the hooker part of the movie), with a small blister forming on the heel of my foot because these boots are total bastards to walk in, I storm in to find whoever has the clue, as I'm pretty sure Steve isn't planning on touching any of my fingers with his ring in a nursing home where a lady is continually shouting, 'SOMEBODY COME!' from her bedroom. I find the clue – another fucking death arrow with another scroll: catch a ferry (that sounds excessive but I live near the coast and catching a ferry is like going to the Co-op for a bar of Dairy Milk and a pack of sanitary towels) – and I start to resemble the Hunchback of Notre-Dame as I feel like there are hot pokers up my toenails.

I get to the bar named on the scroll to find my mum. I walk up to her and my precise words are, 'You absolute whore!!' She smiles and replies with, 'You look nice. Take a seat – I'll order us some lunch.'

Yes, Sue, I am now pigeon stepping around like something out of *Night of the Living Dead* because by now I thought my new fiancé would be balls deep with me wearing my brand-new sparkly diamond ring. In that moment I was thinking, 'Shit the bed, it isn't happening, and my mum has the absolute worst taste in giving me a Christmas surprise.' One hour later, having begrudgingly inhaled a chicken wrap, looked through every single variation of M&S high-waist pants and waited for my mum to take the longest piss in the public toilets, I drag my foot behind me, pretty sure there is now blood, as I catch the ferry back, two arrows hanging out of my handbag like I'm about to go hunting in the outback, with my mum, who seems to be nervously tugging on her oversized bag, which until now I hadn't really noticed.

'Laura, darling, don't be angry …'

I sigh, for the longest moment. 'What now??'

And she reveals ANOTHER arrow. Fuck MY LIFE!! This shitstorm isn't over. And so there I am, back at my nine-year-old Fiat Punto with ten miles of petrol left, and I'm having to drive five miles in the other direction.

I arrive, and my dad described my entering the pub like something out of an old Western movie called *Pistols At Dawn* or something. The door swung open so hard and fast that everyone stopped and looked at me.

'Where is it, then?! Where is the other fucking arrow?? What's next?? LONDON??'

It's at this point, I do believe, that after the months of planning to make this happen, they realised it might not be going as well as they hoped.

'Lolly, don't be angry, but here is your final clue.'

GO BACK HOME??? GO BACK FUCKING HOME???

I drive home determined that, as soon as I see him, I'll throat punch him, because I'm now living on a wing and a prayer that I will get home with the limited number of fumes my car is running on.

I open the door and the house is clean, roses all over the floor, and there he is, on one knee, in a suit with a ring box.

And all of a sudden I realise I have been a massive CUNT. I cry, and I cry, and he says, 'Laura, will you do me the honour of marrying me?'

I just nod and he puts the ring on my finger and says, 'Babe, why the fuck have you got to be such an uptight twat??' And then, 'I'm not going to lie, I feel rough as arseholes and I need to go to bed.'

So, I sat at the dinner table, beautifully laid with my favourite dinner waiting for me, and I ate it alone, chuffed to fucking nuts I was finally going to get married, and at no point did I give a flying fuck that he had flu, that he stayed in bed for the whole of Christmas, because after six years of ups and downs he had finally given me a RING!

> *'I was that woman who waited for the appropriate moment to tell him to remove himself so I could lift my naked arse up into the air and ride an imaginary bike in the vain hope it would encourage full-blown impregnation.'*

As you can imagine, Steve understood my passion to be his wife, and within 18 months we were married.

I managed to keep my overwhelming need to be an uptight bitch to an all-time low and we had an amazing day. We were genuinely happy and he absolutely didn't regret any of his decision to marry me, even though I had pushed him to the absolute brink up to that point. We got the wonderful honeymoon to the Maldives, and for the last time in our lives had a holiday that wouldn't consist of feeding another human and wiping not just your own arse, and we sunbathed in silence. No questions ... I wasn't someone's snack bitch; I was just Mrs Laura Belbin with her brand-new husband.

I think because we had been together for so long we had ticked so many of the boxes we'd wanted to achieve, and so the next logical step was to bang out a kid. By Christmas of that year I was starting to feel nutbag-itus setting in. I insisted I didn't want another holiday; I just wanted to be a mum. I knew what it was like to be tired, I knew it would be hard work, but being a mum was something I had dreamt of all my life. Surely it wasn't that hard? My mum and his mum had three kids each, and they seem relatively well put-together, right?! All this 'just enjoy each other' shit was ridiculous because we'd had loads of fun together already. I was quite frankly bored of his company and I wanted to be growing his human inside my womb.

I was that woman who waited for the appropriate moment to tell him to remove himself so I could lift my naked arse up into the air and ride an imaginary bike

in the vain hope it would encourage full-blown impreg-
nation. Steve would lie there wondering what the fuck
he had just had sex with as the occasional fanny fart
slipped out.

We were incredibly lucky; we fell pretty fast, and all
of a sudden I was that person holding the positive pregnancy test, like 'HOLY SHIT, we're going to be parents.
This is AWESOME, I'm going to be a mum.' I was five
weeks pregnant and googling every single detail of what
my tiny little baby would be doing that week. We named
our little person Peanut and that name kind of stuck.

It didn't really take long for me to be a neurotic mess
about making sure I didn't harm the baby. I wouldn't eat
ham, because you know – they say cured meat can carry
listeria and, well, I had overthought the whole cured
thing and declared I just better have none of it, at all.
At one point I believe I was living off of broccoli florets,
bread and butter. I would call our local maternity hospital so often they ended up knowing me on a first-name
basis. I loved this baby so much and I just needed to
keep him safe.

I think I had got to about 19 weeks, and I had got it
into my head I was feeling pressure, like right-in-the-vag
pressure, and so, obviously having done a swift google of
what it was, I declared I must be going into early labour.
I was in such a fluster; I googled the contact number
of Blake maternity and hit dial, my heart racing. I felt
sick. The woman answered and I was off like a speeding

rocket, at 90 miles per hour, the words falling out of my mouth before she had even finished introducing herself.

I had been using descriptive words like 'pressure around my vagina' and 'I've been constipated for days' along with 'my vagina lips feel so swollen' for a while when the woman at the end of the phone, at this point sounding more and more short of breath, shouted, 'PLEASE STOP!!! You've called Blakes Estate Agents and I'm not a midwife!'

The silence was longer than you could ever imagine as my mind replayed every single word I had just used to describe the ins and outs of my vulva, and I replied with, 'Did I give you my name?' She reluctantly replied with a no. I'm pretty sure she was now permanently scarred; clearly she hadn't ever been pregnant because if she had the phrase swollen vagina lips wouldn't have come as such a shock to her. I put the phone down, barely hanging by a thread. Not only was I displaying signs of an unusually fat vag but I could never ever show my face in Blakes Estate Agents for fear they would recognise my voice.

After what was the most traumatic experience of my life, there was actually nothing wrong with the baby. I was fine and clearly just suffering from a case of the big fat lip stings, which, by the way, is pretty common when you're using your body to harvest a baby. Who knew?!

Each week I would read in extensive detail about how big the baby was and what it would be doing and proudly telling people, 'It's as big as a mango this week', while also being mildly disappointed that no one massively seemed to give a pig's dick about the size of my baby. Looking back now, I appreciate it must have been pretty boring when I'd started giving them these incredibly mind-numbing updates when the baby was the size of a grain of rice.

I made Steve gut the front bedroom in preparation, new flooring, lighting and wardrobes, because babies are renowned for giving a shit about that! I primped and primed every square inch of that room like the queen was visiting. I ironed the Babygros (*who the fuck does that??!*), I walked around the room repeatedly, completely unaware that this would be an all-time pet hate in months to come when I had a baby who refused to go the fuck to sleep. I read every single article about what to buy, and I got it – ALL OF IT, even down to every single sized bottle because who doesn't like a cupboard stuffed full of that shit when a baby only has one bottle at a time?

If the articles told me to howl to the moon and wipe my anus around the threshold of my door for good luck and positive vibes you know I was the mental bitch to do it. I would go through random spurts of putting things in order, then feeling my central forehead vein pop out of my head when I'd find Steve had moved it, or for that matter even breathed near it. The 45 muslin squares were neatly folded in colour coordination next to the 79 bibs, all pristine white and perfectly placed.

I was under the impression this would always be how it looked. Wow! I mean, roll forward a few months and that shit didn't even make it to the wardrobe, it definitely wasn't white and it looked a lot like rainbow spew had dried on it before being reused and somehow I had lost 44 of the 45 muslins.

I was so desperate to hold our baby, love them, care for them and I truly didn't care how much sleep I lost in the process (HAAA don't we all think that first time round? What fools), and so I just wished it all away – the lie-ins, the afternoon snoozes, walking around the shops in peace, having a conversation that didn't include discussions about shit consistency and girth – because I was so sure this worry and panic I'd felt every waking moment would totally disappear as soon as I held my baby in my arms for the first time. Well, that was a pile of shit too, because in actual fact you just die a million times over at the sheer level of responsibility that goes with keeping a whole human being alive for the rest of your life. I remember sitting in the hospital looking at Elliott and realising for the first time that this thing wasn't a five-day working week; it was every single hour of every single day. It had taken the upside down fanny cycling, positive pregnancy test, nine months of pregnancy and thirty-six hours of labour to realise this, and it was really, really overwhelming.

Steve looked like he had been involved in some kind of accident, with small pieces of my bodily function attached to him in some way, from my vomit to the blood that was free-flowing from the hole he used to like filling, which now didn't look quite so appealing. He just kind of stood there, exhausted, happy and worried that he needed therapy for watching a human head pass through such a scarily tight space. The moment you become parents for the first time always sounds so romantic, but the wonderful notion it will bring you closer together isn't really the case – no more than 40 minutes earlier he had heard me shout at a consultant: 'Shove your hand in me NOW and pull it the fuck out!' I'm pretty sure at no point did my husband expect to be in the same room as his wife while she willingly offered another man to fist her while he watched. No, there is no level of romance in it, and yet during pregnancy you plan the candles and soft music to breathe through your contractions in the ignorant belief you'll be that one with make-up and a shaved vagina. Nope, not me! I was the one who spewed in her own hair and looked like the girl from *The Exorcist*.

I had spent all this time prepping for the arrival of this beautiful thing that would fulfil our lives until the end of time only to find we walked in through the front door, sat down, looked at him, watched him do the loudest, most explosive shit, only to realise we had nothing to wipe his arse with – because we had got wipes but the hospital had told us only to use cotton wool – and no bed to put him in … Literally no idea what I'd been thinking, but, being the cheap bitch that I am, I'd told myself I didn't need a Moses basket; I would just hold our perfect baby all the time I was downstairs and wouldn't need to put him down. The reality of that ingenious idea lasted all of 40 minutes, because I told Steve to go to Argos immediately to buy whatever the fuck he could that resembled a bed to put our kid inside. I didn't even give a damn if it was a laundry basket, but we needed something and for the love of God get me some cotton wool because this shit seems to be escaping every inch of his clothing! The real kicker in all of it was that we got the baby that absolutely, with a passion, hated his Moses basket. That thing got used twice for Elliott, and the rest of the time I just wedged him on the sofa and put clean washing inside the basket because I just couldn't be bothered to put it away!

> *'Hello, Mum Guilt, what a pleasure to see you here.'*

So, you're in the parenting club and it doesn't feel much different than before except you're twice as exhausted, with less money, a baby who shits more than you had anticipated and you are constantly covered in spew. What a fucking comedown, this is it?? Where are the new mates who invite you round for takeaway and drinks as your baby sleeps like an angel?? Oh wait, you got the baby that parties all night and absolutely fucking hates to sleep, which means you learn to eat with one hand while bouncing a pissy baby on your lap and singing an old Bob Marley song because it's the only one they like. Yeah, that invite – it went to the parents who looked a lot less feral and a lot more together than we did. Elliott screamed from 10pm until 3am; we hated him, let alone anyone else. I imagine it's the noise they play on repeat in hell to punish someone to the point of being completely demented.

We were the parents who lived by Google. Do you demand feed? Or schedule feed? Ask Google! Do you burp them for ten minutes or forty minutes? Ask Google! Invariably, no matter how many ways we tried to research it, it all came back to the same thing: follow your gut, because these demanding little scream machines don't actually follow rule books, much like us adults, and yet there we are expecting them to fall into a Gina Ford routine by day three and getting our tits in a twist when they don't. No matter what, you aren't getting it wrong because you are continuing to try, and, really, that's all that matters. Something doesn't work, and you've given it a good try – fuck it, try something different. If getting your baby to sleep means you hum the theme tune to *Cheers* while playing the violin, do it if it means you get some peace. Can't say I would have that much patience, but the point is who are we to judge others for their technique?

Yet there is always one pushy twat forcing their opinion on you like they've found the parenting holy grail, even when things do finally start coming through for you. The baby finally sleeps, they stop crying so much, and you can absolutely guarantee Tina Talks Too Much is going to pipe up that her child had a regression and that your child is effectively a ticking time bomb of doom, waiting, at any moment, to revert back to the non-sleeping arsehole that made too much noise. These babies – while they might be similar, they aren't the same. Tina might be right, but chances are she's a tad bitter and can't just celebrate your mini, yet massively huge, breakthrough.

The worst part about someone else's unwanted opinion is the level of fear it brings you, not only that you might end up like poor old Tina, but that then you start to question if you're getting it at all right. 'Hello, Mum Guilt, what a pleasure to see you here. Aren't you just a well-timed bird shit on your jumper at the theme park! Because parenting isn't hard enough, now let's just think about the fact every other person is doing a better job than you are. What fun!' said no mother ever experiencing that horrific situation of literally questioning everything.

Do I not give enough attention? Do I give too much attention? How can I make tomorrow more fun? Will they grow up to love me? Am I enough? I shouldn't have lost my temper! Do they hate me? Am I feeding them enough veg? I didn't try hard enough! Should have I gone back to work so soon? Do I work too much? The list goes on, and it is endless for every single parent, because you love those kids so much you just want to do what is best for them. We are all living with that level of Mum Guilt every single goddamn day, and, yes, I'm so sorry it sucks this much because you just want your mind to give you a break, but sadly that ain't gonna happen. Just be proud of the fact you are that mum who loves your children so much that you're prepared to constantly evolve who you are to fit around them and be the best mother they could ever ask for. No one will get it bang on every single time – if life was designed to be perfect, it sure as shit wouldn't involve 10cm birthing holes with heads that feel the size of a crater from the fucking moon.

Let's be honest, it's not even that much of a big deal. It's actually only for the rest of your life ...

Dear Mummy- and Daddy-to-be,

I know, the beginning of this journey to become parents is new and exciting. The pregnancy test, the vomiting, being a moody bitch as he wonders if he should go live in the shed (FYI: yes, you probably should) and all the long awkward stares where you are just in between being obviously pregnant and having had way too many Burger Kings for anyone to actually congratulate you – it's just precious. Just remember, in the lead-up to the grand event where you meet your child for the first time: nap, sleep in, and nap again, because fuck me when people tell you it is tiring they mean you'll be so wasted by the lack of sleep your eyeballs will feel dry. Do you know how that feels? No, neither did I until I had a small thing screaming in my ear repeatedly for three months straight.

This thing growing, this life, it will change you for ever and if there is one thing you are going to look back and think the most, it's: fuck, I wish I went to the cinema more, or why didn't we enjoy those nights out where we got to talk to each other about interesting stuff like how much we loved each other. Visit places that don't like children, the fancy ones, where people open doors for you, because soon enough you will be those arseholes that push the

stroller into people's ankles around tight corners.
Revel in the fact your house doesn't smell like old
piss because you have three days' worth of nappies
stacked in the bedroom.

Enjoy the silence, make the most of being selfish,
hold hands and for God's sake just remember ... take
another nap. Those little moments will be gone and
replaced with something awesome, because you made
a kid, but you will miss those little things that felt
insignificant about the life you used to live.

I get this sounds a lot like a horror movie ...
I mean there *are* times when it feels like it, but I
promise you will be alright. You will be greyer, but
ultimately you will survive.

Best of luck,

Laura

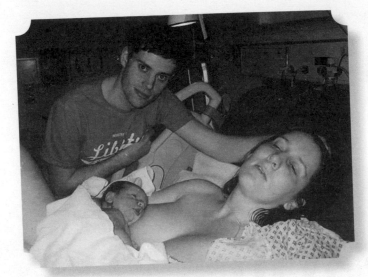

This is the first-ever photo taken of Steve and me as parents. I thought I had my eyes open and was smiling. Someone was also sewing up my vagina. Literally nothing depicts the exact moment I stopped giving a shit quite like this one.

2

Whispers Have you heard of Anusol?

Big bad birthing truths

> *'You might have seen 400 birthing vaginas,
> my darling, but your bedside manner is
> as well put-together as a festering shit on
> the bottom of my shoe on a hot day in an
> elevator.'*

When you left the hospital with the four-winged sanitary towels hugging your gooch and the brand spanking new baby in tow, did you realise how tired you'd be after labour? And when people cooed at your four-day-old baby in the middle of the supermarket, did you ever think you'd be discreetly trying to put Anusol (if you don't know what that is, you haven't lived) into your trolley while feeling like your entire vagina might drop on the floor at any moment?

Nothing prepares you. No antenatal classes, no NCT groups, no peer-to-peer chats. No one really tells you how it's going to go down, or out. Maybe you should have been reading between the lines, though – '36 hours', 'intense', 'sore bum' and so on – but you only truly understand the meaning of going into labour when you go into labour. Why the fuck doesn't anyone actually sit us women down and say, 'Look, babe, sex is great but, fuck me, pushing a baby out of a hole that is absolutely not designed for that kind of girth is going to hurt like a motherfucker. Do not rush into this!'

I can remember the early stages of labour; you know the point: you think you're 9cm dilated but one swift hand up your chuff by a complete stranger confirms you are 1cm and they suggest you go home for a paracetamol and a warm bath. I felt like someone had just punched me right in the face. I get that there is a certain element of truth when they say you're better off at home – midwives see us first-timers day in, day out, acting like the mucus plug falling out (*anyone yet to have a child, that's a visual thought for you to digest*) is like delivering the baby's head – but you also feel like screaming at them: 'TAKE ME SERIOUSLY, FOR FUCK'S SAKE!'

I went home at 6am utterly dejected, with waters that seemed to gush as often as Niagara, which I found fascinating, considering it was squirting out of a 1cm hole! I walked around the house, rocking, holding a puppy-training pad to my vagina and kind of waiting for that moment when it would just happen. They always say you know. You just know when you need to go. Nope! Not me. Let's remember I'm a neurotic nutbag – after the seventh call to the maternity unit in the space of ten hours (*ten fucking hours*), they told me to come back over. Jolly good.

So off I waddled; I felt that if I just went over to the hospital, this kid would slide out like a slippery canoe. I arrived at the doors of the maternity unit acting like the dog's bollocks – I was HAVING this baby now! They checked me: 3cm dilated. YOU HAVE TO BE SHITTING ME. Go back home, they offered. Well, that went down like a sack of shit. I cried and then faked a massive contraction to act like all of a sudden I was now in full-blown labour. It worked – they told me to stay, probably because they couldn't cope with my incessant calling.

By 2am I was absolutely done with being pregnant. I was exhausted and finally I was actually 4cm dilated. Get that fucking epidural in, NOW. I remember within minutes going from feeling like I was about to rip my stomach off to being unconscious. Like, I'm too tired for this, I'm done! What felt like another 900 hours later, having projectile vomited into a water jug, insisted on wearing my odd socks because ... well, I don't even fucking know why ... I was being told to push, with my epidural only half working now and an arse so numb it felt like John Wayne had ridden it throughout the duration of this cesspit of an encounter. I literally thought the devil's horns up my arse must be a walk in the park in comparison. I was wrong, because precisely 2 hours 33 minutes later I was still being told to push and I genuinely thought my vagina might flop out onto the floor with the baby still inside my womb, because this fucker absolutely didn't want to come out!

I can now see the downside to an epidural, because there is nothing quite like one half of your body screaming how fucking painful something is, while the other half acts like it pissed off on holiday and has absolutely no interest in coming back to actually provide any kind of help. You always hear about those women who have a failed epidural, and you always think poor bitch that must have hurt, while inwardly thinking, 'HA, that'll never be me.' Note to self, never be a smug prick; you never know when it might bite you in the arse.

The male consultant joked about how easy it would be for me to deliver the baby myself. I know, right?! Because he knew exactly what it felt like to have a watermelon hanging out of his bellend while being watched by 12 people with absolutely no dignity left. I can tell you now that if he had, in fact, known what a watermelon piss-hole felt like, he wouldn't have been the one joking about how easy it is. You might have seen 400 birthing vaginas, my darling, but your bedside manner is as well put-together as a festering shit on the bottom of my shoe on a hot day in an elevator. Lesson for next time: don't ever say to a woman that you understand how hard it is; never crack a joke about how we just need to push a little harder; and, for fuck's sake, just know that when my waters squirted all over you it was a defining moment for me. My Niagara gush knew to cover you in my vag juice because you had been such an arrogant wanker.

My eyes were rolling, with chunks of hospital hunter's chicken stuck to my chin and throbbing labia that were about to catch on fire, and with Steve and my mum watching in horror as they heard the final girthy grunts come from so deep within my soul I genuinely think I scared the midwives in the room two doors along, and I pushed him out with all my might.

Finally, his horrifically massive 38.5cm head arrived. By this point, to be honest, with a head that fucking big I didn't have to work any more to get the body out. It was effectively like the parting of the biblical seas, and it seemed my vagina would never go back quite to the way it used to be.

> *'It really doesn't matter how you do it – natural, section, breech, multiples, big babies, small babies: we are all HEROES.'*

I can remember the very first moment I felt Elliott on my chest. He was so heavy, warm and soft. I was beyond relieved that this cone-headed, bloodied chunder monster that had just entered the world was mine to keep for ever. They weighed him and happily announced, 'Mummy, he is a healthy 9lb 3oz.' Fuck me sideways. How can something that big not effectively allow gravity to do its job and just fall out? Was it because I had the luxury of a tight cooch? All those muscles that used to tighten even at the thought of a pelvic floor now officially hung like a dry-cured hanging ham.

All of a sudden I had a deep, unbelievable level of respect for my mum! You, my babe, did this three times. You absolute legend. But also, what the fuck were you thinking? You said it was painful, but I do believe the words painful sum up a sprained ankle, not the equivalent of a meat clever to your clit, poon and bum.

I was the third child, but I was the unplanned one that Mum found out about four months in, back in the 1980s when pregnancy tests weren't cheap and you tracked your periods via the birthday calendar that sat next to the telephone in the living room.

Mum always banged on about how she had Russian flu, and I always knew she must have been kick-ass because she never once said, 'I had flu when I was in labour with you, Laura'; it was always, 'I had RUSSIAN FLU when I was in labour with Laura with NO pain relief.' As if that wasn't enough to cope with, I was also an awkward bastard who decided to be breech. Which is the story of my life, really. I no doubt tried my best to be ready for the perfect execution, but due to unforeseen circumstances I was looking for the wrong hole and got lost.

Mum has always enjoyed telling the story about my birth, even at my wedding. The woman who pushed out her chunky-dunk breech baby with no C-section, arse first, and feeling like Satan's sack was draped over her forehead with Russian flu and no pain relief:

Midwife: Mrs Parker, would you like to know what you had? Take a look?

Mum: Oh my goodness, it's a boy! Thank you, it's a boy.

Midwife: Mrs Parker ... You might want to look again ...

Mum: We're going to name him Paul Eric Parker.

Midwife: ... Mrs Parker, I really can't stress enough how you should take a second look.

Mum: Hang on … it's a girl?!?! But why does
            she have a penis??

Yes – that, my friends, is my birth story. The time my
clitoris was so swollen it looked like a massive dick.
Turns out a breech birth will do that to ya – who knew?!
Doesn't Mum just love to tell that story! Now, being a
parent myself, I get it. Actually we all deserve a medal,
and we should be proud, because labour isn't actually
given enough recognition for how fucking awful it is. It
really doesn't matter how you do it – natural, section,
breech, multiples, big babies, small babies: we are all
HEROES. All that said, I truly wish she could just ease
up on the story about that time I was born with a lob
on, not to mention they would have called me PAUL and
ERIC. Fuck me!

Going through the -sunroof ain't my kinda - fun route

Being cut open in major surgery isn't the
'too posh to push' alternative because having
stomach muscles ripped apart and waiting for
them to knit back together is, I've heard, kind
of painful, especially when you have to use said
wrecked muscles to get in and out of bed to

tend to a baby. We always turn our noses up at women who don't do it naturally, like that makes those who do superior. I'm telling you now, until you see a woman with her tits out, support stockings to her knees and a pair of pants hugging her bellybutton while sobbing because every step she takes feels like her bowels and intestines are about to spill out onto the floor, you really can't judge.

I've seen it first-hand, and it never looked like the easy way out to me. My sister brought into this world the most beautiful nieces I could have ever asked for, and on both occasions her body laboured for hours, she writhed around in pain, while patiently waiting to meet them, only to find, after all those hours, that she was to be rushed down to surgery and given an emergency C-section. She was so upset; she felt at times like her body had failed her. What I saw was a woman who did whatever it took to make sure those babies arrived safely – she allowed her body to be sliced open just to give them life. Wow, aren't we just amazing!!! Probably about time we gave a little more praise to every woman, because this thing they call natural is painful, long and life-changing, physically and mentally.

> *'Some say it's just a ping of magical love.*
> *But sometimes it's a bit more like a nugget*
> *of shit being pushed upstream than a*
> *PING.'*

I think, while you don't realise it at the time, this whole roller coaster of birth is painful, emotional and exhausting, but it's the beginning of your love story with your children. The hideous pain SHOULD make you hate them as soon as they arrive, but somehow it doesn't. You just feel relief, happiness and all of a sudden that massive agony you felt no more than a few minutes ago is all gone. You're just so fucking happy it's over, and then all that is left to contend with is falling madly in love with them ...

And you wait ... and wait ... and you think, 'Fuck?!?! Where is my rush? That overwhelming feeling of utter adoration that everyone keeps banging on about? Is ... this ... it?? Because I think I am more in love with the Domino's delivery driver.'

Some say it's just a ping of magical love. But sometimes it's a bit more like a nugget of shit being pushed upstream than a PING. It took me ages – weeks for Elliott and months for Toby. Some people say they connect with their children in the birth canal. I didn't connect with anything in labour other than my gas and air. But don't panic when this sticky, gooey thing appears and takes their first breath on this planet as you look at it and feel nothing. I promise you it will happen, it will be worth it and you aren't a bad mum for taking a moment to find that connection. The most wonderful things that come in life don't come easy, and being a new mum is one of those things.

I remember Elliott smiling at me for the first time. I was in the middle of a shopping centre, he was about nine weeks old (the prick smiled for everyone else but me at this point) and I cried because it felt so good. I felt a stitch more bonded to him in that moment, but it wasn't a ping of instant love because he then screamed the whole way home in the car and I wanted to face-plant a bed of stinging nettles.

The 3 Bs and the 3 Ps

In amongst the carnage of life, finding your feet while feeling a million eyes on you, judging how well you are coping with this new level of responsibility, is your body. Wow, it hurts, right? The veins, the chafing and the rubbing, the long painful exchanges where you look at it in the mirror and see one massive bowl of jelly that used to be your stomach, and it's covered in bright-red stretch marks that look a lot like the road map to hell. You saw Natalie four doors down just snap right back into those size 10 jeans, while you're still reaping the rewards of those tit-height maternity leggings.

I'm going to break down some basic facts about your body after you have a baby. You aren't Natalie; she could be eating grass and snorting cucumber juice for all you know! She might have been naturally thin but she still shits, pisses and farts all the same. Our bodies are all doing things at different times in different ways. No matter how you do it, there are some things you can always guarantee: the 3 Bs and the 3 Ps. Let me give it to you straight.

The Bs

Blood – You aren't dying, I promise! This is just what an angry uterus emptying out its discarded contents looks like. It makes a heavy period look like a paper

cut, and, yes, those maternity pads feel like a wedge
of cheese rubbing against your thighs as you sway
to and fro with a baby that doesn't like to sleep. You
don't quite understand how going through labour, no
sleep and baby blues isn't enough, and that now you
are expecting to become a shareholder in Always
sanitary wear because you're getting through them
as fast as your shitting baby gets through nappies.

Breasts – Yes, you used to be aroused as your
partner tweaked them like the on/off switch to the
DAB radio. Now they're leaking at the sound of a
baby crying and your nipples are like hot pokers
that burn as soon as any kind of pressure is put
against them. Everyone is telling you breastfeeding
is the most natural thing your body can go through
as you place savoy cabbage in your bra and feel like
the veiny, exhausted version of Pamela Anderson.
The idea of him tweaking those bad boys makes you
want to drop-kick him where he stands.

Burning bumholes – Ouch! Your rectum is in
a permanent state of emergency. It looks like the
anus of a baboon with diarrhoea and feels like
razors every time you sit down because you have 40
stitches up it. You can't trust a fart because it feels
like the whole anchorage of your intestinal track is
about to flop out into your leggings.

And the Ps

Pain – You know when something hurts so much but
you're already committed to the situation, so you just
sit there, desperately trying to draw strength from
somewhere? The stitches look like Frankenstein's
monster's face, and every time you piss it's like the
long slow sting of a UTI that just doesn't seem to
go away, mainly because your entire garden pretty
much got massacred. If you haven't ever got to that
point in your life where you have to give yourself a
pep talk then I don't believe you've suffered the pain
I'm talking about. You know, that 'Come on, Laura,
you can do this. You are so brave … it's almost over
now. You are a brave, brave girl' kind of pep talk,
like your mum is sat next to you talking you through
taking a shit and wiping your grief-stricken vagina.

Piles – Because when they said arse grapes, they
really weren't kidding. They just hang there, all
proud and purple. The difference is you have no plans
to take them to your sick nanna in the hospital to
wish her a speedy recovery. No, no, the only person
who gets to enjoy those fuckers is you. They slowly
start to shrink, but after a session of googling you
realise that they will probably be back. Fucking great!

Poo – Oh, the fucking joy! You down lactulose
like your life depends on it, praying it turns your
shit into a brown slip and slide that will just fall out

pain-free. You sit and wait for that moment to arrive like expecting your least favourite aunt on Christmas Day, because not only are you utterly petrified of your baboon's arsehole, you are also pretty sure your vagina is being kept together by a single string of dental floss that could pop at any minute. Know that even Natalie, the size-10-jean-wearing, smoking-hot-ass new mum, is also moments away from shitting out her colon.

It's also at this point I'm going to say, for every single time you get out the bath and your vagina opens like the mouth of a yawning gorilla and gushes water like a burst water balloon: don't panic, I've had a word with some people – turns out it's quite normal. If you are as relieved as I was to hear this, then you're welcome. I was carrying around that bucket vag secret for many years before admitting it was the least sexual gush fest that I've ever encountered. And more often than not it's the only action my vagina sees.

> *'The first time Steve and I had sex again felt a lot like losing my virginity. I lay there, rigid with the fear of the unknown, as Steve nervously looked at me, saying, "Are you sure you want to do this?"'*

I felt a weird pressure to get back into riding the pogo stick. I heard all the stories of women who were banging

their husbands in the hospital hours after birth. I heard
of the ones who fell pregnant again within days because
they were so sexually deranged they couldn't contain
themselves. Yeah, that wasn't me … six weeks post-
birth, I toyed with the idea of his penis and still politely
said, 'You can give yourself a posh wank', because there
was no way I felt ready to even think about that level
of intimacy. It scared me so much because I really felt
like, if it went in, out would come my entire reproduct-
ive system, which would then grow legs and move into
someone else's body. I had been stitched and I was
exhausted, and unfortunately for Steve when I'm tired
he has as much hope of a cheeky poke as I do of seeing
Henry Cavill naked in my bedroom. I wasn't sexually
turned on by the idea.

It's like, when I left the hospital a new mum, I picked
up my dignity at the door but forgot my sex drive was
sitting under the bed. Shall I go back and search for it?
Is this normal? There was that horrific conversation
where my mum offered support by saying, 'Don't worry,
darling, you might not feel anything for a while but eventually you'll enjoy sex again', and I shuddered from my
inner core outwards because A) I didn't even mention
my sex drive to my mum and B) I now know my mum
enjoys sex with my dad. Something that all these years
on still makes me retch a little.

The first time Steve and I had sex again felt a lot like
losing my virginity. I lay there, rigid with the fear of the

unknown, as Steve nervously looked at me, saying, 'Are you sure you want to do this?' Under the duvet, with the lights off and making no eye contact. It wasn't as bad as I thought, but, honestly, since having the kids, it's been a bit like dipping in and out of converting to a nun. I have really struggled, especially since having Toby, to be sexually charged like I used to be, and that has been a massive issue for me. I've felt ashamed and I've felt like there's something wrong with me.

Thankfully Steve is fully committed to wanking silently in the shower and has never pressured me, made me feel bad for this battle with my sexual libido and has always been very patient. Something I am so grateful for because he can't begin to understand the turmoil my body has been through, mentally and physically. Men don't feel the change, other than loving a new person in their life. But for the woman getting over labour isn't a two-week jobby; it's months, and months, and months. So yeah, we are going to yoyo through our sex lives and we shouldn't be ashamed of that.

I have never been that person who has had sex just to keep my husband happy, and it's actually really upsetting to know how many women do because 'my husband has a high sex drive' or they 'worry if I don't he'll have an affair' and even worse still 'I don't have a choice'. When I was in school I learnt in detail about the male orgasm and boys' wet dreams. I learnt how to put a condom on a cucumber (that's a fun one when all the boys think you're an ugly munt, stood in the class with frizzy hair and buck teeth). Would you like to know what I learnt about female orgasms? How to put a tampon in without it getting stuck … Oh yeah, wait, that isn't an orgasm.

I grew up blissfully ignorant that women had those wet dreams, even though in my mid-teens I woke up in the early hours one morning having had the most erotic dream about the boy in school who had the worst acne – I just put it down to being secretly in love with him. I assure you, I really fucking wasn't, but how was I to know that an erotic dream was a normal thing for a girl?? We were told it was a boy thing. Those painful lessons about sex ed it was all centred around the man's pleasure; never ever the woman's. This is absolutely fucked! We all understood how important it is for a man to finish off. That we should lie back and let them get it over with … WHAT???

Where was the woman in all of this? As a society we have been conditioned to believe it is more important for a man to have the pleasure and the woman to come (literally) last. I am not of this opinion. My sexual desire is just as important as his. So, yes mate, we gave you a new kid, and somewhere along the way our need for your penis anywhere near us has kind of dropped off the radar, and you will have to get over that. Do not tell us you deserve the attention and DO NOT ask what is wrong with us, because we are not your sex slaves. We just gave you a new thing to love, and we're finding our feet. While we tread this unknown road why don't you throw in some romance, remind us how much you love us, and never ever think asking for a blow job as we cook dinner is appropriate.

Yes, there are going to be those women who are back on the sex pony within days and they are going to be this vision of utter sexual radiance who seem to absolutely love how highly sexed they are while telling EVERYONE how highly sexed they are, but you aren't wrong for not being ready. You MUST take this journey one step at a time, and find your own sexual satisfaction. Remember you are important in this part of your relationship and DO NOT be rushed back into it.

It is so easy to compare yourself to those other mums in every single aspect of motherhood, especially if you're a first-timer. It can be such a tough road because you literally have no idea if you're getting it right.

None of us ever do, though. It is, without a doubt, like taking a wild stab in the dark and wondering what you hit first while praying it's not someone's face, but you will get there. These babies really don't come with instruction manuals, and it's the biggest shock to learn that they're all unique. Just like us, in fact.

Whether it be a vag birth or a C-section, we are all the most incredible human beings because we created a life that we then basically risked our own lives for. Birth isn't a walk in the park, and yet because it happens every single minute of every single day we all kind of take it for granted. We tell ourselves it's alright, because women do it all the time, but actually our body grew something from a foreign object. It fed it, nurtured it, and when the time came it opened up like the mouth of a terrifying monster and spat it out into the world. There is no easy way out, there are no short cuts and there aren't any pedestals for who did it best. This thing is fucking painful, and actually we should all take a moment to pat ourselves on the back, because we made it through something no man could cope with.

(There you go, I said it and there is fuck all you can do about it because this is my book, which makes me smug as fuck.)

-Laura's Life Lesson - - - - -

My babes, you aren't going to get it wrong. Be sure to take this superpower that is called motherhood and proudly wear its cape, because all the time you try, all the time you show love and all the time you protect them, just know you are doing the most incredible job of keeping that baby alive. You are the mum they always hoped for and, yes, you will make mistakes, but that's the glorious reality of life. Sometimes we learn the best lessons from our 'oh fuck' moments.

what they didn't tell you

* Yup! That thing can stretch like the mouth of a whale and clap back like a saggy pair of curtains. You truly don't get the relevance of a baby's head circumference until you've pushed one out of your hoo-haa.

* You just spent 40 hours of your life you'll never get back assuming every single position that under normal circumstances looks a lot like kinky sex only to find this baby isn't coming and you have to have a C-section. Fucking great.

* So, you have a vagina that is throbbing harder than Ron Jeremy on the set of a porno and you absolutely couldn't take any more if you tried: don't worry, though, you're probably going to projectile vomit too. Just because Why. The. Fuck. Not! The human body. It's a total prick sometimes.

* It's going to feel like someone just booted you right in the chuff. Like a David Beckham World Cup kick and it's going to hum like a rotten songbird for a while. You're going to be okay, though, because you're trying to breastfeed and that means you can take paracetamol ... that really renowned drug for doing fuck all for pain.

* WE'VE GOT A BLEEDER! Are you slowly bleeding out vaginally? Or is this actually the

longest period known to man?! The bleeding will last weeks. Why? Leaking milk from your tits just isn't enough.

❉ It might feel a bit like someone shoved a massive piece of roast beef between your legs that will then rub against your thighs, but I promise it's just the swelling that has effectively made your lips scream at you, 'WHAT DID WE JUST DO?' Don't panic; lip shrinkage is just around the corner.

❉ No one will ask how your vagina is feeling! There won't even be a box of chocolates delivered to show respect and condolences for all the times you won't be able to jump on a trampoline carefree again. You won't mind, much. But, seriously, it will look like a car crash!

❉ You'll be asked if you're doing your pelvic floors 30 minutes after you've had your baby. Smile and nod. But, at some point, you might have to try to work out if you've potentially shat yourself without knowing.

❉ So while you feel like someone just yanked your womb out, swung it around their head a few times and then shoved it back in, be sure to remember that tiny little fleshy thing that was very recently hanging out in your womb is going to want your full attention. Turns out bed rest isn't part of the protocol for having a baby!

❋ Your partner is going to want to familiarise himself with IT again, and you're going to question if you'd prefer to be a lesbian.

❋ What was once a beautifully kept garden will become The Forest of Tangled Pubes. You might need to comb it before it turns to dreadlocks.

❋ When you go for your first walk, smile. But know that inside you'll be crying because you think your ovaries are sliding out like a slippery eel.

❋ People are going to be begging you to visit, to cuddle the baby and tell you how bloody awful the next 20 years of your life will be. They'll also come with offers of gifts. Don't let them in. Literally shut the door and live like pigs in poo! Who cares if they're offering you things to celebrate the fact you guys had sex nine months ago. Squalor is king.

❋ Auntie Joyce is going to offer to make you a dinner. FUCK YES!! Do not politely decline, remind her not to forget pudding!

❋ You will cry. Over random stuff. Like a leaf just fallen from the tree, the milk on the cornflakes being too cold or how you can't poo without it feeling like a million needles stabbing into your bum. Trust me, those tears are real and you absolutely need to know because hormones are a bitch and they make you question everything.

❋ Sure, you wonder how the fuck Sally Sunshine with her tinsel tits and perfectly manicured nails is making this whole thing look easy, with her ten-day-old baby, as she tells you she doesn't feel tired and took just 20 minutes to push the baby out. But trust me, babe, that poor bitch just needs a hug, a strong coffee and enough time to tell you she's currently in a shitty place (literally) because she has the worst case of piles.

❉ Someone at some point is going to say the words: 'You only had a baby. Lots of women do it.' It's quite possibly going to be a man, and, yes, you have my full permission to drop-kick the prick straight in the nuts and be sure to tell him, 'What's the big deal?? They're just bags of hairy skin. Every man has them.'

❉ So what if you don't want to leave the house! Put Netflix on and for the love of fuck do absolutely nothing but eat shit, laugh, cry, and enjoy the utter hot mess of your house.

❉ Be kind to yourself. We forget the trauma, because as a woman 'we must bounce back', but Fuck That. I didn't bounce; I tripped, fell and rolled down a very large hill and yet I still made it to the other side. Just find all the moments to give yourself a gentle but firm pat on the arse and remind yourself what a fucking incredible thing you just did.

❉ At some point or another you might be mental enough to do it all again.

The good stuff about birth...
(yes, there are good bits)

- That moment when it feels like you're pushing out the biggest shit of your life is weirdly satisfying even though it's a massive burning hole of doom. You make the same noises of a satisfied porn star being finger blasted only without the orgasm.

- They will be smothered in bloody vag juice and a little bit of poo but you won't care because you're going to kiss them, repeatedly. Not even remotely bothered by the fact you have faecal matter across your face.

- They will fart and you will smile because nothing has ever sounded that cute.

- Those midwives, they just kick ass, don't they? When you say you can't do it any more, like a massive sisterhood they cheer you on and remind you how awesome you are.

- Tea and toast. Nothing else needs to be said other than how post-birth it's the absolute dog's bollocks.

- You'll leave that hospital a new woman, not because you're a mum but because you did it!

You FUCKING did it and that makes you the biggest, baddest bitch-ass boss ever. You fought through the pain, you believed enough in yourself to bring this life into the world.

✳ Epidurals. Who knew that one little thing could be the most precious gift that keeps on giving. It takes the pain away, you chill out, maybe a little crossword, why not throw in a snooze, all the while your body is attempting to exit a melon and you don't feel a fucking thing.

✳ You might hate him, but he was kind of cute when he stroked your head, and when he cried the moment he saw his child for the first time. Actually, you all of a sudden love him a little more because he's helping you to the shower and telling you how proud he is of you.

✳ You will look at them for hours; it will feel like days. You did that! You are awesome!

✳ Yes, sometimes it will feel a lot like you have no idea what's meant to be happening. Go with it; none of us know what we're doing, and that's okay.

✳ It's the only time in your life when you'll happily hold conversations and eye contact with complete strangers over what weekend plans they have while they try to figure out how they sew up your arsehole.

❊ You are going to count their fingers and toes,
repeatedly. Bit like that scratch card you
didn't win on; you keep checking just in case it
changes. It's because this whole thing feels a bit
like a Lotto win.

❊ Your heart will grow a little bigger in a way you
didn't think was possible; you will carry that love
for them until the day you die.

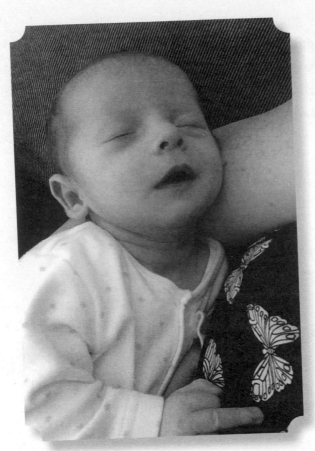

When all those mums told you being exhausted is worth it because you'll always love your baby, and you're two days in, wondering if it's acceptable to ask the midwife if they can put it back because this shit is way too tiring.

What the fuck have we done?

Life with a newborn kind of sucks

Did you hear the other mum say, 'My baby feeds and then lies down and sleeps for five hours at a time' while your eyelids were stapled to your forehead to make sure you don't fall asleep behind the steering wheel? Is it safe to say your baby screams every single time you try to have a poo without them? Is it also safe to say that they only sleep on you, or if you rock them into submission?

I'm going to take a WILD guess and say exhaustion hit you in the face like a steaming bag of baby shit dropped out of a second-floor window. Right?

Fuck knows how I remember this conversation because my knuckles had been dragging along the floor for months, but when Toby was a few months old I remember sitting at baby weigh-in chatting to this mum. The conversation went something like this:

Her, washed hair, no pouch: Oh, my girl is so good. She slept through from nine weeks. She does twelve hours and she always just goes down in bed with no fuss.

Me, smelling of BO, with so much talc in my hair I must have looked like I had been caught up in a drug deal gone wrong: Whore.

I kid you not. I called her a *whore*.

Safe to say the conversation with her ended there and then, no swapping numbers and hugging it out.

Truth is I couldn't handle hearing how this mum had hit the parenting pond like a glorious swan to water while I was a one-legged pigeon trying to swim. I needed to speak to the mum who was as tired as me, who was struggling just as much I was struggling. I needed that mum who was on the verge of crying because then I would have realised I wasn't alone.

Was I alone? No! Absolutely not. But I wish someone had been there to say, 'Hey, me too! Let's sit together and rest frozen peas on our vaginas and celebrate how little we have our shit together.'

Although I was very much winging the shit out of what I was doing I was slightly more together than Steve, who looked a lot like someone had just shoved a dildo up his arse and told him to hold it in. He looked permanently shocked and scared shitless. He had never held a baby before, let alone changed their nappy, and he absolutely didn't expect the level of tiredness (do any of us??) The day we brought Elliott home, I sat in the back of the car, looking like roadkill as Steve gingerly navigated the motorway as if he was carrying a weapon of mass destruction in the back. We arrived home only for Steve to try to parallel park the car like he stole it, and bump up the pavement. Instead of doing what normal adults would do and realigning the car, he just got out and went into the house ...

I shouted, 'What the fuck are you doing?', as the nose of our car stuck right out into the road and cars began to queue behind, waiting for Steve to take his dick out of his hand. He reappeared with the keys to the other car we owned looking chuffed to nuts, and declared, 'I'll move the other car!'

I didn't expect so soon into becoming parents to want to kidney jab him with a set of keys, but as I angrily got out of the car and waddled to the driver's side, I truly felt like that was the moment. I had no more than 24 hours before had my vagina sewn up by another woman and I was now trying to park the fucking car.

Worst part was, I moved the steering wheel the opposite direction, pulled forward and the car was parked. He just stood there awkwardly trying not to make eye contact with me or any of the pissy drivers waiting. He was sleep-deprived, and so worried about breaking this baby, but thankfully babies are pretty robust!

> '*If you're reading this wondering if you're the only mum in the world with sandpaper for eyeballs, a broken baby, a bikini line hairier than a chimpanzee's chin (don't worry, it's nothing a good bout of Veet won't fix), stop. Fuck the perfection.*'

Sleep deprivation is used as a form of torture in war-stricken countries – fuck me, I get it now. Throw in a baby and you really will send that prisoner over the edge, because when a baby hits that certain pitch of cry at 3am, you really do contemplate headbutting a wall to drown out the noise and hopefully fall into an unconscious state that requires a hospital admission (but doesn't leave you with any lasting brain damage).

'Oh, babies just eat, poo, sleep, repeat …' Why did no one tell me that they only sleep for 20 minutes at a time?? When does this stop?? Don't tell me I'll eventually get my sleep back. I am a woman on the edge and I need realistic timescales. My baby is singing me songs of his people throughout the night and I've been told I should sleep when baby sleeps, but it's frowned upon to sleep behind the wheel of a moving vehicle … I need hope and a light at the end of the tunnel, none of which needs to include the words 'it could be months' or, worse, 'years'.

I agree, babies shit a lot; they like to eat a fair bit, too, but none of the earth dwellers that came from my body liked to sleep as babies. They loved to exercise their lungs, especially through the night when I was more likely to fall into a narcoleptic suicidal state. Someone told me Mary Poppins was in town but short of doing fucking smoke signals from my back garden with the living room rug I was pretty sure the bitch wasn't going to show. I was fucked if there was someone else out there worse off than me because I smelled like dried milk and fried onions and I officially had a crusted left nipple that clearly hadn't seen a flannel for a week or two.

So, if you're reading this wondering if you're the only mum in the world with sandpaper for eyeballs, a broken baby, a bikini line hairier than a chimpanzee's chin (don't worry, it's nothing a good bout of Veet won't fix), stop. Fuck the perfection. You will get through it. There are others out there just like you ... like me ...

> *'Then, like some mystical beast from the deep, you begin to notice the ever so slight glimmer of hope ... Did they just ... nap for A WHOLE HOUR??'*

Being a new mum was a lot lonelier than I expected. Everyone talks about the friends you make, which you do, but where are they at the 2am night feed? Where are they when you're sat in your PJs, alone in the morning, with no one to pep talk you into getting dressed and facing the day? You have to silently navigate all those times alone, and you don't realise how many there are until you find yourself sometimes never actually seeing another human being all day who doesn't demand to be fed and need its arse to be wiped.

You're always told that once you have a child you will never feel loneliness again. That is utter bullshit, and those people have clearly never tried to have a conversation over whether to have a brioche bun or a seeded bagel with a six-month-old. Just to confirm, they don't fucking answer back! (Not to mention, brioche buns taste like soft arseholes.) I think that shockingly shit insight into motherhood meant I fell with a lot more of a thud than I had expected. Babies aren't fulfilling company and I can't say toddlers are much better either.

In fact, nine years into parenting I'm only just starting to reap the rewards of a child that actually understands jokes and is able to engage in a relatively enjoyable conversation.

I felt a lot of the time like I needed to be that person who just owned it. I didn't – do any of us? I'd like to think not. We know this thing is meant to be natural but it feels back-breaking, and when you are in amongst all those other mums, who wants to be the person who sticks their hand up and admits they cried during the night? Or that they haven't washed for days? Or that they talk to themselves? You just don't, because you worry that will lead to rejection. But I'm either fucking mental (kind of a given) or that is all of us! Please, tell me, for fuck's sake, that it is all of us.

Then, like some mystical beast from the deep, you begin to notice the ever so slight glimmer of hope ... Did they just ... nap for A WHOLE HOUR?? ... Wait ... they just lay on their playmat and entertained themselves for 17 whole minutes (who knew 17 minutes felt so long??). And you are beginning to regularly clean yourself to the point that perfume and roll-on isn't needed to cover up your BO any more. You are beginning to flourish into this world of motherhood! Fuck Mary Poppins, she isn't needed; you are owning this shit all on your own. Is it because you're now so exhausted that your standard for a successful night's sleep is a long blink?? Or is this kid finally starting to talk your lingo?? Either way, it feels fucking great. You can't help being silently smug at that mum with a four-day-old baby at weigh-in with eyes like piss-holes in the snow. You can foresee the journey she has ahead; you feel sorry for her, but mostly you're just so fucking pleased it's not you.

> *'The simple act of pushing past my fear and showing up to a group of strangers, praying they weren't part of the Cunt Mums Club, meant I actually found help in the most unexpected of ways.'*

I remember starting a baby group with Elliott when he was three months old. It was recommended by the health visitor because it was officially confirmed that I'd gone batshit and actually this was a good thing for me, forcing me out the house. I rocked up utterly petrified, with sweaty palms, praying Elliott didn't scream the entire time. I wanted to make a good impression on these women – in my head I was walking into a room full of my future friends. I sat down. I looked sheepishly at everyone, some already talking to each other, and I prayed they would be just like me because my loneliness bordered on painful. I wanted to be in a group of women who understood exactly what I was feeling in that moment.

Well, Elliott had successfully saved up four days' worth of shit for that moment. Yup! Four whole days of rancid shit, pumping out of his arse like a brown fire hose, extinguishing the belief in my soul that I actually had a chance of making friends. I looked at him in utter disbelief. Now?? FUCKING now?!!

But that little weekly check-in with those mums became my saving grace. I would count down the days until I could go back. No one cared about the old gigantic shitter, Elliott. I was included and it felt so good. Thank fuck it wasn't just me! We met up most weeks; sometimes we'd go for lunch. We came from different walks of life and we all had different views, and we all struggled in different ways, but one thing we all shared was that we were all exhausted and desperate for some company.

The simple act of pushing past my fear and showing up to a group of strangers, praying they weren't part of the Cunt Mums Club, meant I actually found help in the most unexpected of ways. I am thankful for that group of strangers sat in a circle waiting for the first one to pipe up with the first, 'Hello, my name is ...' It made my first 12 months of motherhood so much more bearable. I think initially it felt a lot like I was totally alone but I came to realise actually sometimes you just have to do a little bit of digging to find where the help is – look for the support groups, where you will, without a shadow of a doubt, walk away with at least one friend.

> 'You're going to be judged either way: the
> mums who ask the breastfeeders when
> they're going to stop; and the bottle-feeder
> who get shitty looks for whipping out a
> bottle of Cow & Gate readymade. I am yet
> to figure out how this has anything to do
> with anyone else.'

The lovely thing about the group was that some breastfed,
some bottle-fed, and guess what – we all just got along.
The fact we chose different paths didn't mean we had to
judge each other. The Bottle Vs Boob debate absolutely
grips my shit. My darling, this baby is mine and I am
absolutely mindfucked as to why you feel it has anything
to do with you whether I put a teat or a tit in its mouth.

You're going to be judged either way: the mums who
asks the breastfeeders when they're going to stop; and
the bottle-feeder who get shitty looks for whipping out a
bottle of Cow & Gate readymade. I am yet to figure out
how this has anything to do with anyone else.

Breastfeeding is so hard. I have the highest level
of respect to anyone who works through those initial
painful weeks, the dedication of it never being a straightforward latch. Babies with tongue ties, boobs that don't
produce enough milk and having to pump around the
clock, cluster feeds, cracked nipples, the list goes on
and on. You are amazing, and I will always support any
mum who chooses to breastfeed. The fact that feeding

in public is considered controversial in this day and age is an outrage. If you have a problem with a baby breast-feeding in your local restaurant, I have a problem with your gingivitis lips around that glass of wine – go drink it in the toilet and then tell me how fair that seems!

Sadly, I have seen some of the most horrific things said about bottle-feeding mums. My journey of becoming a mum had a lot of bumps along the road, which meant a lot of things didn't go to plan. Breastfeeding my children was one of those things, and I am not ashamed now to say they were both formula-fed.

But I did feel so ashamed for such a long time. I felt like I was the bad mum when people asked how long I fed for and I replied: one week. Breastfeeding is so hard. Through people close to me I've seen how hard it is, and the work, time, effort and patience it requires. Lacking a bond with my babies only made the idea of being attached to them for that long even more difficult.

You can say women lack support across the board in this country. I agree, we do completely lack that guidance, the resources are stretched and you receive next to no aftercare because the midwives are understaffed and in hot demand. When I had both of my children, the support was minimal and yet the pressure from others was immense, and I was the mum desperate to breast-feed but with absolutely no knowledge. The basic truth is what I do with my children has literally fuck all to do with you. 'Fed is best' – that's all that matters: it just comes down to the fact a baby that is fed, whether it be breast or bottle, is the most important thing. And don't give me this shit that this phrase is controversial; it's simply about making sure your baby is fed and alive. The only controversy I see is when I read women online saying that bottle-fed babies will get cancer and die, that if you don't breastfeed you don't love your children, that formula babies should be taken into care, we lack a strong bond and that we are lazy mothers.

The problem lies directly with people who feel entitled to an opinion on something they know nothing about – the rape victim, the woman who has a nipple phobia, the lady whose baby was tube-fed, the mum who didn't have enough milk, the mum with multiples or the mum who just didn't want to! The list is extensive, and actually they're all valid reasons, because we chose what was right for us. I was the mum who was heavily medicated and my breastmilk would have killed my children. Remind me again how 'fed is best' is such a bad thing to say? You say informed is best; I say the only information I needed back then was from a medical team who knew how to make me better, and actually your negative shit over the years has damaged me beyond words.

When I gave up with Elliott, I was heartbroken, but I was also emotionally broken. I was told to call a breast-feeding expert in our local hospital for advice on how to quickly and effectively give up breastfeeding. I couldn't gradually reduce breast pumping until my body adjusted and eventually stopped making milk. I needed to go cold turkey and stop it immediately.

I called – she was expecting me – and when I said that I had no problem with producing milk, I was like Daisy the cow, her response was: 'Yes, Laura, and that is what I find so disappointing about you. There are mothers who would do anything for your supply and you are just going to throw it away without even trying.' I think those words will haunt me for the rest of my life. I sobbed because the medical professional who was meant to be helping me was condemning me as a bad mum – or that's how it felt. I wish I could speak with her now, tell her about my journey and remind her that words can be harmful. I would like her to see Elliott aged nine, incredibly healthy, happy, loved – *that* is the priority of raising children.

I was trying my best to stay alive. Actually, I was doing everything for my child to just be there as his mum. The next time you go to judge that woman who formula-feeds, think about all those times you have felt prejudice over breastfeeding your baby, think about how that made you feel, and then do us all a favour and focus on your own journey as a mother. The only important thing you should do is raise that child to be kind and caring, not judgemental and blinkered into thinking there is only one way of doing things in life.

It's 2020 – there doesn't need to be debates on who's doing it better. There just needs to be a league of women supporting each other because life is tough enough.

> *'Elliott wanted to be a big brother right up until the moment he became a big brother and then he realised, "Actually this is totally shit. That thing makes noise all the time and you never seem to put it down to pay me attention."'*

You think having a baby is hard, but when that baby has an older sibling who is now looking at you like 'What the fuck have you done??' because this new baby has totally ruined the perfect little vibe you had going and they detest the idea they now have to share their time with you, that is hard. Elliott wanted to be a big brother right up until the moment he became a big brother and then he realised, 'Actually this is totally shit. That thing makes noise all the time and you never seem to put it down to pay me attention.'

I remember Toby being six days old. You can imagine the state of us. Steve and I were half dead and Elliott, who was four and a half, was demanding every single ounce of our attention. Bedtimes were horrific. He wouldn't eat what we gave him, he stopped wiping his own arse, he would wet himself. I get it; that was his way of saying: 'I need more attention. I am so lonely and sad … please help me through this.' Sadly for him, his parents only had the most basic of instincts, which was to keep him alive by feeding him, washing him and putting him to bed. If he did anything that diverted from that plan then, well, quite frankly he was fucked!

Elliott walked up to me and said, 'I just put something in my ear,' literally as I wiped his brother's shitty arse, with bags around my eyes that hung past my vagina. 'What?' I said in complete confusion. In his hand appeared a small foam shape from the *CBeebies* magazine my mum had bought him to keep him 'entertained'. 'I put one of these in my ears!' He was actually proud of his arsehole achievement.

Steve and I had decided we absolutely didn't give a flying pig's dick about online advice – we had tweezers, we were getting this thing out ourselves. Forty minutes later we arrive at minor injuries because all we'd managed to do, as Elliott had wriggled and moaned, was lodge it further in. I was fucking livid. The nurse tried, he cried, I insisted. The nurse tried again, he cried and she said you need to go to hospital. 'I'll call them to say you're on your way.' You can imagine that drive can't you? Well, as Elliott smugly looked out the window, having his little jaunt over to the big hospital to see the big doctors, I genuinely contemplated leaving him in the hospital car park because he was making my life a million times harder.

We arrived – he skipped in holding my hand, like the cat that got the cream, as I dragged one foot behind me like Edgar from *Men in Black*, and the newly qualified doctor (Dr Jack, never forgotten his name) explained the whole process. Wonderful; now get the kid on the fucking bed, I want to go home, I am too tired to care. Elliott cried. The doctor suggested I get on the bed with him and I begrudgingly agreed. Again they made no progress. Dr Jack said we might need to bring him back tomorrow for a general anaesthetic to remove it. I don't particularly remember the words that came out of my mouth, but it was strong and very forceful because he called the lead consultant, Dr Tickle (*mate, I will tickle your balls if you get this thing out of my kid's ear*), who said, one last try, and I begged Elliott to just not be a cock and sit still. At no point did I admit that we had actually made this worse ourselves – we 100 per cent blamed Elliott for how deep it had gone. The only saving grace of being a grown-up is that you can blame your kids and there is literally nothing they can do about it.

Dr Tickle freed the foam piece of crap, which, thanks to his sleep-deprived parents who refused to admit they had done anything to make it worse, had been stuck so far down my son's ear he almost needed fucking surgery to remove it.

Elliott took to being a big brother very slowly, and while I hear so many stories of parents who say their children loved it the moment their brother or sister arrived, just know they don't all cope that well.

I mean, Elliott is a shining example – struggling so much with it that he would voluntarily shove something into a hole just to get more attention. The only level of enjoyment he got out of Toby was the fact he would suck his nose, something that started out as cute and then ended up being a logistical nightmare, because as soon as I left the room Elliott would have his nose in Toby's mouth so much so he'd end up with a love bite.

'You are your baby's biggest expert; always remember that, and trust that instinct when things don't feel right.'

I have been told the jump from one to two is the hardest, but considering my intro into being a mum of two was like walking through razorblades barefoot, I was never willing to find out how it could get easier with a third baby. Newborns look cute and wonderful on paper and the amazing thing is that, with time, you completely forget how horrifically exhausting it is, which means you are lulled back into thinking a newborn is a good idea.

Some people love them; I personally like holding them and giving them back, because I also know they come with a whole list of responsibilities, which includes washing bottles, changing repeated shitty arses throughout the night, rocking a sleep-resistant baby so much the floorboards begin to sing their echo-y sighs as you repeatedly pace them, and keeping up-to-date with the most recent government idea about what we should be doing. One year we're told co-sleeping is a massive no-no, then the next there is a whole article on how to do it safely, while in the next breath you are told to use dummies and then quickly told they are a terrible idea. You have to work out what it is you want the health visitor to know, just so she doesn't lecture you on all the ways you aren't doing something they have now been told they need to push.

As I had had two babies four years apart, the advice and guidelines I was given completely changed. The 'absolutely under no circumstances do you make a bottle up in advance' had changed to 'you can put one in the back of the fridge'. I was encouraged not to rock Elliott to sleep, and was told it was a great idea with Toby. I didn't need to bath Elliott every day and yet now with Toby I was being told I should. Fuck my life, no wonder mums walk around utterly petrified over what they should be doing – it changes weekly. I understand a lot of that comes from research and understanding babies better, but it also means we can never truly be sure what order it all comes in. The one thing having a second child taught me was to just do my own thing – remember those pieces of advice if I felt unsure, but also know that one kid hadn't turned out too badly (minus the foam-shoving crisis), so I could be pretty sure I could do it again with some degree of success.

Nothing will prepare you for it, no matter how many times you birth them. They are all so wonderfully different, and even in those early days they tick differently to any other child you will have.

No centile chart, health visitor or GP can tell you what is best for that baby quite like you can. If motherhood was a qualification it would be a degree. You did nine months of studying, you sat a really fucking long, painful exam, and then you learnt on the job how to fit into the shoes of this career you chose all those months ago.

Sure, everyone is going to pump you full of what worked for them, even when you didn't ask for it. Don't worry, it's okay to get pissed off with that. Smile, nod and let them think you give a shit while inwardly working out what Chinese you'll be ordering that night. You are your baby's biggest expert; always remember that, and trust that instinct when things don't feel right. Never feel like an overanxious mother and be proud of this new level of awesome intuition – it's one of the cool perks of the job.

-Laura's Life Lesson - - - - -

When you see that woman standing alone at the baby group, the one who doesn't make eye contact and you assume she doesn't need a friend, just go say 'hi'. Chances are pretty high she went there in the hope of finding someone to talk to and now all of a sudden she feels like a loose dick at a party who doesn't know how to leave without making a scene because she has one baby hanging off her tit and a toddler that's screaming for a snack. She needs you. Be the friendly 'hello' or the 'don't worry my kid's a prick too' in her life to make her feel less alone. We all need that person.

Sleep when they sleep, and other lies

----

* Yes, that is literally all they do. Shit, feed, scream and maybe, if you're lucky, sometimes sleep. Everyone missed out the bit about the lack of sleep, didn't they?? I know, what a bunch of pricks!

* *It goes by a lot faster than you think* ... Um, Yeah. Not according to my wrinkles or eye bags.

* *Sleep when they sleep.* THIS DOES NOT HAPPEN FOR EVERYONE.

* *You will love every second.* If you sit alone and feel like the only mum totally hating this whole experience – don't worry, me too.

* *You'll become so good at multitasking and being on time.* Liars. You're going to be late! All the time. Fuck anyone who has a problem with it, babies will take shits at the most inconvenient times.

* Nanna Pat is going to tell you she used to wake up before the baby to boil the nappies and get ready for the day. Remember she also had her kids 900 years ago and her rose-tinted view on what life is like with a newborn is about as much use as a cock-flavoured lollipop.

❋ *You can have sex after six weeks.* Not so much
a lie, but fuck me you're probably not going to
want to. Trying to have sex again is like slinging
a cat up an alley. You have absolutely no idea
what is going to be dragged back out afterwards.
Don't worry, though, because if you want him,
and he manages to sling it past the dry-as-a-
nun's-chuff exterior, you're probably doing better
than most.

❋ *You can't get pregnant while breastfeeding.*
Yeah, those 15 kids running around screaming
… those are hers. All of them! She doesn't
own a TV, her husband needs to find a hobby
that doesn't include her vagina and she's been
breastfeeding for 19 years.

❋ *Don't rock your baby; it'll learn that's the only
way it can sleep.* Well, you know what I say?
Rock the baby. If that's the only way you will
get to eat your dinner before it's stone cold then
who gives a shit. Little Johnny isn't going to
require rocking at age 16! The whole 'rod for
your own back' springs to mind, yes? Shove it
up their arse. You can't make a rod, but you can
absolutely do whatever it takes to survive.

❋ *Babies need a routine from day one.* Yes, and I
need a holiday on a beach with Brad Pitt as my
personal chaperone, but that ain't happening.

✻ *Only feed them homemade, organic, vegan-friendly, soya-alternative, with a shot of kale.* OR … go to the local supermarket, buy a jar and feed your baby because truth be told that little bundle of joy gives no shits how you fill their tummy.

✻ *Breast-fed babies can't get wind.* Having had a colicky baby hang from my own tit, I can confirm they scream just like a bottle-fed baby.

✻ *Your baby should be doing XYZ by now.* Your baby might not hit the milestones when they should, but I also don't manage to take a shit every day. And you don't see someone measuring the square root of my arsehole. Don't worry, they will get there in their own time.

✻ *Mum knows best.* Yes, you do! So when you worry something isn't right that doesn't make you overanxious. Ignore the online forums where they say singing church hymns at the full moon helps a baby's fever. Use the inner mum in you to know when it's time to see a professional.

✻ *Breast is best.* NO. Happy mum, happy baby. Do what is right for you, not what everyone else thinks is right.

✻ *You'll love your baby the first moment you meet them.* Or it might take a month. Don't panic. It'll happen at some point. I guess it'll be worth the wait!

* *You lose most of the weight.* Who gives a shit if the latest celeb mum has bounced right back into her size 8 jeans and you're six months in, still wearing your maternity leggings. That bitch makes it look easy because she has a personal chef, trainer and a nanny. Chill, babes, you're keeping another human alive. Eat the fucking cake.

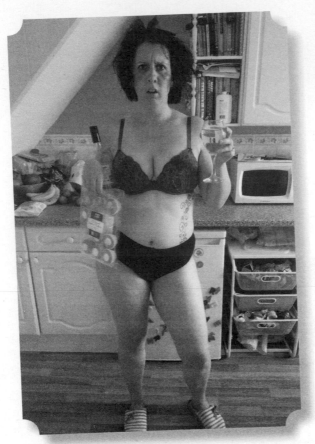

One day I'm going to be skinny,
rich and happy, with tits like a
supermodel. But until then I just
might work on loving myself
the way I am because I'm kind of
fucking awesome right now.

4

Saggy tits and belly rolls

Learn to love the skin you're in

'My life was being wasted worrying that other people might think I was ugly. Truth is, no one could have hated the way I looked more than I did.'

I grew up believing loving myself was easy, maybe because when you're young you just believe, a bit like the ending of a Disney story, that the princess keeps her size 8 waist even after ten kids with a husband who's loaded.

When I was young I was blissfully under the illusion it was normal to love ourselves. It never occurred to me that I would have to work on being the person I always saw myself as – banging bod in a miniskirt. I'm not sure when or where along the way that changed, but in my teens I started to become this person who didn't like her boobs and who tried not to smile because of her teeth. She would critique photos over and over until she deleted them. And soon enough I was a fully fledged adult who totally hated the person she saw in the mirror. How sad!! I was put on this earth (*thanks, Mum and Dad*) to live a life I was robbing from myself. I spent so long concentrating on how utterly repulsive I felt about myself that I hadn't once taken a moment to appreciate how fucking awesome my body was. It was keeping me alive! I was here! And yet my life was being wasted worrying that other people might think I was ugly. Truth is, no one could have hated the way I looked more than I did.

I had these incredible women that I looked up to, my mum and my sister, Emma. Both always reminding me from a young age to know my worth, to understand I was beautiful and that I didn't need a man to define who I was. They were role models to me in many respects, but it wasn't until I reached adulthood that I realised it.

They constantly told me I was good enough, but back then I couldn't move past this crushing feeling that they just said it because they loved me. I'm so thankful to them now, because without those moments where they cheered me on from the sidelines I don't believe I could have become the person I am today. And even now they continue to be the cheerleaders in my life.

I have never been a big person, but the vast majority of my life I have looked at myself as something revoltingly big. (*Never helped by the unrealistic magazine covers splashed across all supermarkets, because you just believe that, to reach any level of happiness, you need to look like the photo of the smiling woman on the front with perfect white teeth and a flat stomach, as she talks about how she found happiness through eating kale for breakfast and daily orgasms.*) My go-to thing when I hate myself or when my anxiety is high is to just stop eating. Food becomes cardboard and I chew it with a constant need to retch because it feels horrible in my mouth. I look fucking great during these days – Jesus, what a banging bod – but fuck what an utterly messed-up bitch I am on the inside. The compliments are amazing, they feel good for a nanosecond, but then I return very quickly to the person who talks herself through hunger pangs by reminding herself how she doesn't need to eat breakfast or lunch. I always get told how healthy I look, how incredible I have been to lose weight so fast. Amazing that, isn't it? That because I am thinner, I am given more attention. Men look at me differently and so in turn that negative cycle of skipping meals continues because I believe it's the way I can stay in control of my own happiness, all the while being utterly miserable. Work that one out?? Actually, don't; you'll be there a while.

I have suffered like this since my early teens. I remember my best friend once sitting on the end of my bed as I went to the toilet and just as I stood up to wash my hands I heard her gasp. I knew exactly what she'd found – the rotting lunches my mum had made for me that festered at the bottom of my bag. Harder to drop a sandwich in a bin than you think when you know your parents will find them at home and your friends will ask you what the fuck you're doing in school. So, they just sat there, all green and gross. I think she maybe found nine.

That was a fun conversation, especially as my dad caught her pulling them out of my bag and then went on to ground me for not eating. Pretty sure a counsellor might have been a better course of action, but it was the 1990s and who the fuck knew how to deal with shit like that? I didn't. It's not like we had the luxury of Google, or forums. We had dial-up, which took 25 minutes to connect, and even then you were bollocked for using it because that shit was expensive. I'll never blame my parents; I was a very troubled teenager with complex issues they knew nothing about. They kept telling me how much they loved me but that didn't change the outcome; I sometimes just couldn't face food.

I then found love, and obviously with that comes a level of contentment and you eat like your life depends on it. All of a sudden that woman with an hourglass figure who stood with not a stitch on was smuggling muffins and rolls, and I'm not talking about the baked variety. My weight has fluctuated since then but not often to any great degree; that is, until things get tough and my old friend Starving Stan appears to keep me in check. We had holidays where I thought I looked hideously fat, but I look back now at the photos and can see I was so thin. That saying 'I wish I was as fat as I was the first time I thought I was fat' is so true.

After I had Elliott I took a one-way ticket to frump town. It felt cosy and safe in my knitted gilet (how the fuck is that a thing??) and jeans that rose so high up my stomach I had a permanent camel toe on show. I had done something amazing in birthing a baby and yet I felt so ashamed of the body that came afterwards. I was 26 but I looked like the hip 76-year-old nanna. My stretch-marks stayed thick and red for longer than I had hoped, my boobs drooped so much more than I had expected and I felt self-conscious when Steve saw me naked. I liked lights out for sex and I didn't enjoy looking at myself in the mirror. I should have been celebrating that

I was doing this awesome thing called mothering, but I was shamefully looking in the mirror at something I just didn't expect. Heidi Klum was back on the catwalk of Victoria's Secret just weeks post-birth; I was in the aisle of Asda looking at my favourite chocolate bars. Getting my body back wasn't high on my list. At all!

I would repeatedly tell Steve I wanted to change. I felt unsexy and insecure, and I would constantly quiz him on whether he was having an affair with someone at work because I felt like such an ugly mess. Elliott was three-and-a-half when I had finally had enough.

'Ask yourself: when you die, would you like to be remembered as the woman who worked hard in the gym but never gave herself a break? Or as the person who just laughed wherever possible, smiled from the inside out and stopped giving a fuck about what number was on her clothes tag?'

I started couch to 5k. I remember starting the first day: run for one minute. Piece of piss! Cue me 30 seconds later blowing out of my arse with lips so white I was beginning to look like Jim Carrey in *Me, Myself & Irene* when he gets cotton mouth. How could running for one minute be that hard? And yet there I was, running slower

than most snails, in my New Look leggings, Steve's oversized hoody, and the same trainers I'd owned for 11
years. The point was, I was actually moving.

Along the way I began to find a level of confidence
I hadn't had before. I wasn't just running along the
alleyways and side roads, I was actually venturing out
onto main roads where people would see me, in actual
running trainers and real gym kit. WOW! I was now officially a runner.

My body was changing; I was getting fit and I was
feeling good. Had my body changed massively? In the
end, yes. But during that process, no, not really, but
how I looked at it had changed. It was one of the first
moments in my life as an adult where I actually loved
it without it coming from starving myself. I was actually being healthy! Looking in the mirror there was
the same woman, but in my mind I saw something
different.

Well, that all went down the shitter as soon as I fell
pregnant again, because then the only running I did was
for the ice cream van at the end of the road. (*Safe to say
I don't even run for the ice cream van any more; I just
keep a well-stocked freezer of Ben & Jerry's and somewhere along the line I've lost one of those brand-new
trainers ... so you know ... that's not ideal.*)

After I had Toby, I was so numb to everything that
I didn't even register if I should have an emotion about

my body. I was jiggly. I can't say that was the most awesome feeling in the world but being the mum of two children I put my own need to look flawless to the bottom of the pile.

Having struggled so much with my own personal perception of myself over the years and then going through a horrific mental breakdown (*don't worry, the breakdown is coming in Chapter 6*) meant only one thing. There was only one way to go, and that was up. So, yeah, my tits touched my bellybutton! I had cellulite all over my thighs and arse! I really couldn't be arsed with the idea of plastic surgery because no matter the lengths I went to in my quest to find this ultimate level of contentment, I would still be expected to do the school run and look after the kids. No post-surgery easing back into life; my life was being a mum so it was about time I owned it.

I started looking at myself in the mirror naked more often – I can't say I even know why, but I just found myself staring. I think at the time I was so detached from life I didn't have a feeling about what I saw. I wanted to love me, I wanted to nurture what I had left and my body was a big thing. I was so desperate to eat again and put weight on because for me it was the beginning signs of recovery. I wanted to be better enough to eat so much that I would gain weight, not often what you expect to hear because we always celebrate weight loss. Not this time; I felt robbed of the things I had stolen from me, things I didn't realise mattered until they were gone, like time with my baby, loving myself and loving life.

As I got mentally better, I felt relieved: I was still here. And I loved me so much for getting through this. While in some senses it took a village, actually it all came down to me! I did it, this body did it. I cried and cried as I started to feel better, in fact I could cry right now because it truly felt like I had, by the tips of my fingers, managed to cling on to the cliff edge of life and claw myself back onto land, and all of a sudden I took this huge breath of relief. And I realised I just didn't give a fuck about holding my stomach in any more, or trying not to wave too hard because my arms wobbled. I found new priorities, and none of them included over-analysing my body like I used to. It wasn't a near-death experience, but it was like a massive twat over the head that made me see things in a new light. I was looking at myself totally differently.

I think the biggest way in which I let go of these inse-curities was posting photos of myself online. To begin with it was just on my private social media page. They were carefully staged, never going too far. I remember posting a side-by-side of Kendall Jenner, freshly woken looking absolutely lush and then my alternative was dried dribble down my face, yesterday's mascara and greasy hair. Then I started my blog, and soon enough

I was letting go of so many things I'd held on to, all because I was taking a risk to post a funny photo in the hope it made someone laugh. I have never been more thankful over something working, because it has in turn allowed me to flourish into a person I never ever thought I would be.

I've never believed in scales; I don't own them – I refuse to because I think they are the devil. They remind us of the things we haven't achieved and guilt us into thinking we haven't tried hard enough when we don't lose or gain the pounds we had hoped. I appreciate a digital weighing tool isn't to blame for that, but it is the catalyst for unhealthy thought processes. I used to fear them because of the numbers I'd see on the screen – I recognise that now, and I have learnt that those numbers don't represent how my clothes look; those numbers don't represent where I find my confidence. I have to recognise that, no matter where I'm going in life, this body is going to travel with me. Sometimes it will be bigger, sometimes smaller, but it will always, no matter what, be this body. It's my only friend that will go to the grave with me, and it deserves respect.

My body doesn't look like how I'd hoped. It's hairier, smellier and it feels a lot less passion than I'd thought it would in my 30s, but fuck it feels good, because I have finally let go of things I realise don't matter.

Ask yourself: when you die, would you like to be remembered as the woman who worked hard in the gym but never gave herself a break? Or as the person who just laughed wherever possible, smiled from the inside out and stopped giving a fuck about what number was on her clothes tag?

I want to always be the second person, because I realise I am not cut out for the perfect life and having the perfect body. Which, by the way, doesn't even exist. All the way down to our toes, everyone has a problem with something. And please do not tell me the rich and famous are content within themselves because sadly they are the biggest advocates of plastic surgery. You see, even all that money, the fame, the fans and success can't bring you happiness if you don't just believe it within yourself first. The tragic reality is they doubt themselves because the media lie in wait for the moment where they get out of a car and you can see cellulite bulging, even though they go to the gym every day. They live with the worry about not looking on point because the whole world is watching and waiting for their next fuck-up – actually, that doesn't sound like much fun! The media has so much to answer for. When we stand in the queues at supermarkets and peer at the latest gossip mag, we see these people at their worst, and we love it because it makes us feel slightly more normal, but it also leaves us feeling completely inadequate because this culture of 'let's poke fun at the fat rolls and wobbly bits' means we then feel ugly for probably having more of an ass than that actress or model plastered over those glossy weeklies.

Those insta-models fanny deep in the Bahamian waters of the tropics have days where they hate themselves, and yet sadly the expectation is they must always look the epitome of perfection. Why? Because sex sells and so they paint their smiles on, they pose on those beaches and they make us all believe they're in love with every single aspect of their lives. Wouldn't it just be an incredible place if we all admitted that those shit days happen to us all? I'm not talking about vaguely mentioning in passing you once might have felt a bit sad about your ankles not looking right. I'm talking: let's just be totally honest.

> *'Believing in yourself is a bit like a diet, lifestyle change, or whatever you want to call it, but the point is it takes work. Every single day.'*

There are days where I wake up and want to cry. I realise I can't see my vagina because my belly rolls get in the way and I wonder if I actually could open bottles of beer with my teeth. Those days exist to remind us we're human and that we have a pulse. It just feels like an utter shitter when they arrive, because invariably they last 14 extra hours longer than any other day, and you sit there in absolute misery.

It can be so easy to lead yourself down a path of bitterness where you start to pick holes in the other people around you, but, truly, does that make you feel better? Maybe for a second, but really deep down I think eventually that feeling of self-righteousness starts to wear thin. How far down the line do you have to go before you realise you aren't happy? How many friends do you need to lose? What self-worth will you lose in the process?

Yes, you might be a size 18 and, yes, you might think that girl who goes to the gym and wears crop tops to the local supermarket doesn't have the same problems as you, but did you ever ask? Or did you assume? How are we meant to be build each other up if all we ever do is make assumptions over shit we are yet to ask?!?! Stop comparing silently, and for the love of fuck just compliment each other. I know! Big ask. But actually if we spent less time giving it the one up, one down and more of a 'Wow, you look nice', you would all of a sudden find that skinny bitch you assumed was a stuck-up whore all because she's naturally small is a fucking riot and you can just be friends.

Babes, I used to want to bounce a coin off of my arse. Well, in actual fact, if you bounced a coin off my arse I'd swallow the prick whole and I now realise that in itself is more of an achievement than a negative. I celebrate the fact we all come in different shapes and sizes. We all yearn for something to be different, but how many months or years is it acceptable to punish yourself for all the things you haven't achieved? No matter how much you hate your body that won't ever change the one you're living in. You are stuck with it until you die.

Sure, have that nose job, book the bigger boobs, have the liposuction but just make sure you truly believe that you are already absolutely wonderful just the way you are. Really focus on the endgame – that tiny nip and tuck, is it the one thing that'll change how you feel about yourself? Or is it the beginning of something that fuels your desire to change other things you all of a sudden find ugly?!? In the words of Coco Chanel, 'beauty begins the moment you decide to love yourself'. How do you achieve that? Well, my version was having a full mental breakdown and blacking out for a couple of months of my life. Can't say I'd recommend that! I would say it's about reminding yourself of the things you've achieved, no matter how big or small they are. They should always outweigh the things you are yet to tick off your list.

Believing in yourself is a bit like a diet, lifestyle change, or whatever you want to call it, but the point is it takes work. Every single day. I will spend the rest of my life reminding myself how far I've come, and when I feel a little bit like a dog just shat on my face I will remember the girl who just couldn't ever take the compliment or believe what people said, because she's come pretty bloody far. There is no one sure quick fix but there are millions of ways to try. Do it however it works for you:

- Therapy
- Naked star jumps in front of the mirror (do it at least once in your life)
- Joining the gym
- Doing couch to 5k
- Stand in front of the mirror and give yourself a minute to look (*don't go grimacing as you read this. I see you!*) – you are AMAZING!
- Writing lists of all the awesome shit you've achieved
- Talking to yourself (*I do it every fucking day*)
- Doing that naked photoshoot (*go on. I dare you*)
- Being patient
- Finding kindness

Above all else, even on the days when you don't want to, be sure to say to yourself: 'I love you'. You have to do it, because one day it will sink in, and what have you got to lose? Literally nothing but the two seconds of your life it takes to say it.

So what are you waiting for? The world to tell you they accept you? Because, my babes, you'll be waiting a lifetime on someone else's approval when all this time that thing you need lies right within your own mind.

> *'Do me a massive favour and just live! That involves eating. It also involves sometimes wearing the clothes you had hoped you wouldn't end up in. But, to be frank, you aren't changing today so put it in the "fuck it" pile and move on.'*

Don't punish yourself by sticking photos of the skinny version of yourself on the fridge to guilt you into not eating that cream cake. You know as well as I do you're going to eat that cake. You have two choices: you either look at skinny you while stuffing your face and utterly hate yourself, or you enjoy every single inch of that cake, smile and remind yourself life is for living and some of the very best things have come from making mistakes, taking wrong turns and learning that sometimes we will take steps backwards to then find the strength to keep stepping forward. Eat the fucking cake; the heavier you are the harder you are to kidnap!

The fashion industry is changing, but at the same pace as a tantric orgasming slug that hasn't shot its load in a year. In short, it isn't fast enough. There really doesn't need to be a slow integration of varying sizes, it's this simple: have the catwalk filled with women of every size – small, medium, big, short, tall. And we want cellulite, we want natural, we want curves, we want age, but most of all we want real. The fear is it'll put men off, that they won't want to see that. Well, quite frankly any man who can't appreciate the female form in all its glory should probably shove his dick in a meat grinder that doesn't stop turning until it falls off.

I am sick of society telling us sexy and beautiful is one kind of woman. I want to see mannequins that aren't unrealistic. I don't want to see the dresses and jeans for the curvier ladies hanging off those plastic statues made of nightmares (their faceless heads just follow you everywhere), all baggy and loose. It leads us to believe that if we fit those clothes currently clinging to old Plastic Penelope for dear life because she's clearly nine sizes smaller, we'll just look like her fat friend that no one invited to the party. I don't understand why this is so hard. How can we still be fighting to see a better range of clothes in our every-day stores? With mannequins wearing normal sizes? Rather than companies only providing the one slight model with those awkward hands where they look like they are showing you that operation on their carpal tunnel (*who even stands like that?*). How can the short girls, tall ones and big ones be told that no clothing store stocks our size? Why? I'm not fucking Bigfoot!

I have to be that person who orders online and hopes that one thing I now have to wait five days for to arrive doesn't look like a hot mess once on. You will take my money, my hard-earned cash, as I order multiple sizes and varying styles because I don't know what will fit and how it'll look. All because we just don't stock for my people. I don't get given the same luxury of your 'average girl'. I look pretty average, no third leg?? Nope, I've double-checked! I also don't have a third or fourth tit, but because I have big bangers I also can't buy bras unless I drive to the back end of beyond to find somewhere that can accommodate my size. Really guys? REALLY??

So, here we are, considered outside of average, with a heavy dependency on carbs and a false illusion that we will absolutely start the next fad diet just so we can fit into those jeans, or look better in that bikini because we just don't have the body ... yet. Once we have achieved that diet, though, you can bet your arse that you will then say you'll be happy once you've toned up, but then Christmas arrives and all of a sudden you're nine roast turkey sandwiches down and that pair of trousers don't do up any more. So we find ourselves in the same depressing position of believing that once we finish the diet all will be good again, until we then remember about the gym and so on, and so on.

Do me a massive favour and just live! That involves eating. It also involves sometimes wearing the clothes you had hoped you wouldn't end up in. But, to be frank, you aren't changing today so put it in the 'fuck it' pile and move on.

The industry of women we see on magazine covers, catwalks and plastered over every shop isn't going to change the way we want it to right now, so it's time we changed how we look at our own journey. It's time we broke down the importance of those goals and made them realistic. It's important we all – women, men, young and old – provide a place within our community where we choose acceptance and don't have to constantly battle the idea that those people who don't know us are entitled to an opinion over how our body looks. That goes for women labelled too skinny as much as it does for the women called too fat. We aren't 'too' anything; we're just who we are in that moment, and at some point or another it will change, but why chase the endless dream you aren't ready to follow and punish yourself along the way?

I can never get back all those times where I hated myself for being bigger in the face, or for the rolls of fat that sat over my jeans. I can't and I no longer want to go back to any previous bodies. The ride this body and I have been on has been awesome – sometimes it's meant an abundance of food and other times it's meant I've barely eaten, but it all makes up who I am right now.

'Beautiful is every single shape and size. If you want that fitness dream to come true, or those size 10 jeans to slide, then you deserve that journey to your goal – but it's so important to remember to be kind to yourself along the way.'

We need to look at how we see diet and exercise; none of it should include being shamed into doing it. I know of doctors who blame every single big woman's problem on their weight. While they might have a point, extra weight puts additional pressure on everything your body has to cope with, but actually how do those words help someone? How can a sprained ankle be turned into a weight issue? A person who is within their BMI could be eating pure crap from takeaways and instant meals but you never preach to them because they 'look' healthy. It's not okay that someone leaves feeling less of a person than the one who walked in that door for help because she's called fat by a medical professional. The fitness instructor who puts unrealistic goals in place only makes that person feel like they're failing before they begin. And then asking them to shamefully list all the foods they shouldn't have eaten but did anyway? How is humiliating someone allowing them to accept themselves right now? You can't build someone up by embarrassing them. You can't encourage someone by shaming them.

Actually the current state of people having such horrifically low self-esteem only confirms that. A rough statistic says that only 2 per cent of women believe they are beautiful. More than 60 per cent of girls as young as ten suffer low self-esteem. That means before they even begin life as adults they already believe they aren't good enough, they are already telling themselves they aren't worthy, that they're ugly, and tragically, with such a tiny percentage of grown women loving who they are, it means there's a much tougher example for these kids to follow. I was that girl in the 60 per cent category, but I am the woman who is happy with the body she has, who is at peace with the way she looks because I can see that, no matter how I try to change what I have, self-acceptance is so much more powerful than any Botox or boob job.

I promote body beautiful. Beautiful is every single shape and size. If you want that fitness dream to come true, or those size 10 jeans to slide, then you deserve that journey to your goal – but it's so important to remember to be kind to yourself along the way.

Steve and I are bringing our children up in a very open household when it comes to our bodies. The kids see us naked – it isn't a big deal until you make it a big deal. I don't want them to grow up expecting to see in a woman what they see in filtered and airbrushed images. To be quite honest that's only going to lead them on to a life of disappointment! Beauty is only skin deep, but when you have an expectation of something, having waited literally years to see it in the flesh, only to find it has cellulite and stretch marks, that might be a big shock. I don't want that reality for my boys, but more importantly I don't want the women or men they end up with to be faced with that level of rejection or humiliation.

If as an adult I have at times struggled to separate the difference between fact and fiction on the web, how the fuck do we expect our kids to do it?!? We can't – it's impossible. We can't expect schools to teach our kids why things like belly rolls and boob sag are normal and beautiful. We can't rely on the internet to be a daily reality check because that ain't ever gonna happen and we absolutely shouldn't leave it down to them to navigate alone.

My boys are going to be swamped with images of men they wish they could look like, and women they wish they could get in the sack. I need them to truly understand that even those luscious-lipped, ripped-torso sex bombs don't actually look like that away from the camera. I hope my kids grow up knowing that maybe they don't look like what they had expected but that doesn't make the version they are right now wrong.

-Laura's Life Lesson - - - - -

That compliment on the tip of your tongue –
about how that dress looks nice on the mum in
the playground, the lady who braved the gym and
got fit, the woman who got the haircut she was
so nervous to have – just push past that awkward
feeling (you know the one I mean, the one that
makes your vagina tingle out of fear they might
chin you and tell you to fuck off) and just give
the compliment. The reality is, you won't get
chinned; she isn't going to tell you to fuck off.
In actual fact, she'll be chuffed to the nuts that
you even noticed. Chances are also high that she
hasn't been told in a while either. Be a legend and
spread the love.

PS If you do get drop-kicked in the chuff,
please don't hold me accountable.

Dear Perky Tits,

Well, turns out it didn't matter really! Did it? You
know, the tiny waist, tiny arse and blow job lips.
Growing up I always promised myself to be the best,
the most glamorous and the one with the hot bod. I
promised liposuction when things started to enter the
cottage cheese stage. I swore I would get a tit lift as
soon as I popped out those kids I was desperate to
have. I didn't do any of it, which also included that
gym membership – babe, it turns out even adult me
fucking hates exercise. All those times I faked an
asthma attack in PE back in school should have been
a warning sign that the treadmill wasn't for me.

Being the super-glam hot one seemed so
important, but it turns out that involves getting up
before the alarm goes off and holding your stomach
in whenever you're around people. Why, though?
For who? Because I'll be fucked if I'm getting up
before any alarm unless it's to go on a holiday with
a 24-hour buffet.

What I'd do to just go back to you, the 17-year-old
girl who thought she was the ugliest, fattest, least
likely to ever have a penis near her vag, and say:

Don't worry, babe. It's coming. All the lads who
called you ugly and told you what a mess you looked,
they actually don't matter. Yes, you will never

experience a tit wank over the local park bushes
with a bottle of 20/20 in your hand, but I am led to
believe you truly won't miss out on much. Be proud
of all the venereal diseases you missed!

I want to hug you so tightly and tell you that
you're not alone. I want you to see all the things
you go on to achieve with that body you believe isn't
good enough. I want you to see where we've got
to now, all tit loose and fancy free. Why? Because
I remember looking in the mirror and seeing
something grotesque; now I wish I could have seen
how tight my arse was back then and I truly wish
I hadn't taken that for granted. Mainly I want you
to love you because you were fucking fabulous
back then, even as that awkward teenage girl who
designed the whole movie poster for your GCSE art
with the words SCREM because you're dyslexic and
forgot the A. (Didn't matter, truly, but I understand
how that wasn't the most incredible moment in your
life at the art open evening.)

Eighteen years on from that fragile girl who
constantly asked Steve if he was paid to date her
– because I truly couldn't believe my luck that a
guy actually fancied me – I now see how sadly
insecure I was and how desperate I was to be
loved by someone. If only, my darling, you could
have loved yourself first, believed in who you were
before anyone else and just known that, no matter

what, you were good enough the way you were. You
deserved that moment, you were worthy of that
life, and, while it has taken a moment longer than
it should have, you did eventually arrive at your
destination. I can't repair the old wounds, but I
absolutely can bravely and loudly wave our flag high
in the sky. I do it for every woman, but I particularly
do it for you – the Laura who 18 years ago was too
scared to stand up and be counted.

Look at us, we finally made it. I stood up for us
and I believed that we deserved to be counted. I am
proud of where we ended up and how hard we had
to work to get here. It has been worth every stumble
in the road and every challenge we've overcome.

Thank you for being you, even when you didn't
feel it was enough, because, without those moments
of self-doubt and reflection, it wouldn't have led me
to this moment in my life.

The early stage is all shits and giggles. Then you fast forward a few years, knock out a couple of kids, and it turns into all giggles, until somebody shits.

So this is happily ever after ...

Relationships

> 'So many people have babies thinking it'll
> bring them closer together, but never in
> the history of life has a hanging ham vag,
> leaky tits and eyes like piss-holes in the
> snow brought anyone closer together.'

Steve is my wingman. He's not one of *those* dads that are about as much use as a cock-flavoured lollipop. He actually parents and doesn't use the words 'I have to babysit my kids', a saying I truly do not understand (they didn't complain when they were balls deep). And yet even now, in this day and age, there are men who believe parenting is about throwing in the occasional 'listen to your mother' and 'go to bed'. I kind of hate those types of men; while they think they've been at work all day 'slaving away' and deserve downtime because they have to leave the house, the poor bitch who ruined her vagina to bring them offspring is slapping at the grass, tired, lonely and feeling useless. Where is her night off? When is it her time to feel like what she does is fucking amazing? When will they see all she does for nothing, including wiping a kid's dirty arse more than once a day.

These guys, they give the good guys a bad name. But Steve, he's a keeper. And he puts up with a lot of shit. Doesn't mean we don't bicker as much as the kids, or that we don't push each other to the absolute brink of wanting to punch something. Eighteen years will do that to someone, and I'm still trying to figure out how the fuck we've managed it for this long. The noise he makes when he chews is so obnoxiously loud that I wonder how the fuck I haven't stabbed him in the eye with my fork. I love him, but, fuck, sometimes I loathe him.

We are always evolving to make it work. Every relationship goes through those periods where it's just touch and go, where you lose each other, and having children is a prime example of those times. So many people have babies thinking it'll bring them closer together, but never in the history of life has a hanging ham vag, leaky tits and eyes like piss-holes in the snow brought anyone closer together. It's the natural way of making sure you very rarely have sex, and feel exhaustion on a level that makes you wish he'd just worn a condom that night nine-plus months ago. It never, ever brings you closer together because relationships are hard and being a parent is hard, and the combination of the two is fucking hideous at times.

Managing a relationship in the early days of having a baby is a bit like being in the middle of a really loud storm; you know he's there because you can see him amongst the chaos, and yet he feels a million miles away. In between being absolutely fucking exhausted, there is this tiny little thing that is 50 per cent him and 50 per cent you, which is slowly but surely managing to drive a wedge between everything you always knew. Sex is a no-go, dinner on time is a distant dream and the only physical contact you have is when he touches your shoulder to tell you it's your turn to change the shitty nappy.

Relationships in the early days are sexy. They're pretending you never fart while feeling like a helium balloon that is desperate to deflate. They're never complaining about how badly your vagina is chafing because you've had sex 14 times in one day. It's fun and free, and the love feels overflowing. How can you love someone that much and they don't even annoy you? Then you grow more comfortable and you let out a cheeky parp to see how it goes down, while still being desperate to impress all his mates and his mum and still never complaining about the fact your vaginal wall feels like it is haemorrhaging all-natural lube with every single sexual encounter you have because you're still riding high on that honeymoon sex that never seems to be enough.

I can remember the early days of my relationship with Steve and saying to his mates I didn't mind him going to a strip club. They all patted him on the back, like, 'Good man, you've got a good one.' Yeah, I never wanted to be that woman who says, 'Go on a lads' holiday', followed by, 'if you want to be put through the seventh circle of fucking hell because that is where I'll send you if you think about going.' Thankfully he hasn't had the desire to either go to a strip club or on a lads' holiday, and I'm never sure if it's because he just loves my company or is utterly petrified of what that level of hell looks like. I never expected to be that wife, but fuck me I really am. I'm sure there are plenty of women who happily wave their partners off to go on week-long holidays, but the idea of it makes my shit twitch, because I've already thought about all the ways I wouldn't want to empty the bin and put the kids to bed alone for a whole seven days.

The younger me, pre-real man and absolutely all about the fictitious boyfriend I made up in my head as I spoke to my Boyzone poster, thought I would be that woman who did 40 lengths in the swimming pool before jogging home, making dinner and giving nightly blowies, fantasising about how many other men would wish they had me. Roll forwards to now, and I'm that woman who takes her bra off before sundown while forcing a whole pack of chocolate digestives down her throat (then writhing around in pain because it turns out nothing good can come from 5,000 calories in 15 minutes), watching Netflix as he sits there and wonders if you farted a little? Or burped? Either way it stinks.

His level of patience exceeds mine, which, depending on the time of the month, really isn't hard because I can feel an overwhelming need to smother him with a pillow when he snores at night. He can sit and listen to my endless nags, bitches and moans, piping up at appropriate moments to confirm he's still invested in the conversation, although I feel pretty confident, having been with him for this long, that he's probably thinking 'shut the fuck up'.

He listens to my incessant noise about how I think he will run off with someone and how I will utterly despise him for it, all the while knowing I am about to build myself up into a complete state of jealous rage and start crying because I have now imagined the whole thing happening where I grow old and lonely. He hears it a lot because sometimes it's really hard not go to this place where I believe all the bad shit will start happening. You know, like: 'Things have been going well for a good while, I do believe it is about time we went to disaster zone, emergency meltdown and assume everything is going downhill, and the very best way to ensure that happens is by making up a whole romance in my head between him and a work colleague.' I'm not being funny but you haven't even been in a long-term relationship if you haven't secretly stolen his phone to check through his entire WhatsApp messages, call history and all other messaging facilities. If you are a man reading this, yes, I am telling you now she has done this. Don't hate her; she is a neurotic nutbag who loves you, but, well done, you've passed the test and not been caught out, which means you are still in full ownership of both your testicles.

People often tell us we are 'couple goals' on my blog ... WELL. About that! This whole road to being the couple we are now kind of had a few of hiccups along the way. As in, I split up with him, broke his heart in two, which led to him having a minor 'eating disorder for a bit' hiccup ... Oh yeah, we are totally couple goals ...

I was so young when I settled down with Steve. We moved in with each other when I was 18 and quite honestly we were inseparable – sounds great but in actual fact four years later it was kind of stagnant. We lived for getting stoned every weekend and drinking ourselves into alcoholic comas. We would be wrecked until around Wednesday, when the taste for the party life would once again tantalise our taste buds even though we had promised ourselves a weekend off. There was never a weekend off, and actually it meant all we lived for was being a fucking mess. I just felt like this relationship was pretty old, and I was growing out of it really fast. I remember telling him it wasn't working any more and he pleaded and begged me to not end things. He was crushed – to be honest, so was I! He wasn't the kind of bad guy you hear about – he loved me with all his heart – but I thought at the time I had lost my love for him.

My parents barely spoke to me; they couldn't understand it. How could I leave him? He was a good guy! They were heartbroken he wouldn't be part of the family any more. I lost drastic amounts of weight by skipping meals – my all-time favourite way to feel like I was in control of my life. I looked good; actually fuck it, I'll say it: I looked amazing. We moved out of our rental property into our respective parents' houses, but while we were doing different things in different ways we still seemed to be tied to each other. I spoke to him a lot. Sometimes he would call me in tears, begging for me to take him back, and I would have to put the phone down. It hurt that I was hurting him this much, but I enjoyed the attention I was getting from other men.

This was the girl no one looked at and all of a sudden I actually felt really sexy and it was a whole new world. I think this phase is called selfish twat-head, but I was experiencing something I had NEVER experienced before. I hadn't realised I was attractive to other men who weren't Steve. And actually the saddest part was that skinny me who was inwardly broken got more attention because she looked on the outside more pleasing on the eye. Not sure why I felt like that was the better alternative to having someone loving every single inch of you for just being you.

Have you heard of the grass always looks greener? Yeah, it really does, doesn't it?! I started to bury the pangs of feeling that I might be missing Steve – he had now told me that staying in contact with me was hurting too much and he needed space. I understood and didn't see him much, but I did miss him. That's weird, I thought; maybe this is how a break is meant to feel?? We had been separated for two months now and I hadn't really seen him for a good month of that.

On 15 January, the anniversary of the day we started dating, I woke up and the hurt in my heart was so heavy I couldn't string two words together. I was dating someone else at the time, and I remember driving to this bloke's house thinking: 'If when he opens the door I feel something I'll know I don't need Steve and I have to fully commit to removing him from my life.' I arrived, the door opened and all I thought was, 'I wish you were

Steve.' I just knew it was wrong that I was now string-
ing another guy along. This wasn't me! This wasn't who
I was. I didn't fuck with people's emotions and I knew
what I wanted. I needed Steve back, but at this point I
had no clue if he would have me back.

Having apologised to the new bloke for being a monumental douchebag, I got back in my car and raced along
the motorway with the song from *Notting Hill* 'Gimme
Some Lovin'' ringing through my head (I always loved
that film), tears streaming down my face, knowing I had
to try to get Steve to take me back.

Reaching his dad's house, I asked Steve to come for a
drive with me and he hesitantly agreed. He was so thin.
So very thin, and the sadness just sat around his eyes;
the pain I'd caused had left him looking like half the
person I had broken up with two months ago.

I took him down the beach and I begged him to take
me back. The worst part of it all was I knew he would
take me back because I knew how badly he loved me
still. Even after all the hurt, all the anguish, he just
wanted me. It all sounds so wonderful and romantic,
but, when you love someone, putting them through that
level of pain isn't something you ever forget.

He promised things would change. We wouldn't party
like we used to, we would focus on our relationship
more, but most of all we wouldn't lose each other again.

All of a sudden my parents were talking to me again,
my dad was in tears, my mum hugging Steve, and I just

stood there like the adopted child that no one actually liked as they welcomed him back into the family.

We were taking things slow, easy, finding ourselves again. No sex, just talking and being together. He had arranged a date. A bouquet of flowers arrived and I wore the sluttiest underwear, shaved every inch of my fanny and knocked back a glass of Lambrini before the taxi arrived. He was wearing a suit and he took me out for dinner (in the hotel where I thought he would fucking propose but where I instead got that pissing arrow). I got drunk wwaayyyy too quickly, as a family of eight celebrating Nanna's 90th sat next to us, listening to me slur the words, 'I am sssoooo going to suck your dick in a minute.' Steve said to this day he has never felt or heard a silence quite like the one in that moment. He felt awkward. I was smashed; I didn't give a shit.

We went back to his dad's house and heavy petting quickly ensued as I stifled the occasional fizzy pre-spew burp bubbling under the surface. I was now just in this red lace bra and thong (*my body was banging*) with a pair of thigh-high stockings. I slowly unzipped his trousers, I teased him, rubbing myself up and down him like a rampant dog over the local park shagging all the bitches.

All of a sudden I realised something was hurting, OUCH. What the fuck was that?? Steve went to sit up, I yelped with pain. 'Holy shit, what is it?' he said, panicked, and reminded me his dad was downstairs watching *Who Wants to be a Millionaire?* and to be quiet. I peered down and to my utter horror I had done such a fantastic job of shaving my lips that the streamline effect had caused my vagina to become entwined with Steve's open zipper. I was fucking stuck to his jeans by my hairless left flap.

To conclude, we didn't have sex that night, but we did spend 15 minutes of our lives trying to detach my minge from his trousers.

I'm not sure if that was the defining moment where we both realised we were destined for each other, but it definitely showed we worked well together as a team.

The damage that had taken place over those two months was plain to see in Steve. His clothes hung off him and the person I once hugged was now a lot smaller, his ribs were visible, his hip bones protruded and he admitted he'd stopped eating and started exercising because it was the only way to help with how badly life was hurting. I was responsible for that and there hasn't been a moment since where I have taken the dedication he has for our relationship for granted. It took him a long time to put weight back on and, while he was desperate to, it also took him a long time to trust me again. I didn't blame him; to hurt so much that you give up on life runs pretty deep. We are now 14 years on from that time and I can still feel the pain from seeing him hurt like that.

> *'He's considered patient and amazing,*
> *while I'm just labelled lucky. Hang on!*
> *How is that even possible? Owning a*
> *vagina doesn't make me a second-class*
> *citizen.'*

During the times I haven't been with Steve, just before we met and during our separation, I have encountered men who haven't treated me well. They threw me away like a rag they were finished with. These men are the bad boys that most girls are drawn to, and yet we all know they aren't the ones who will make us happy. We weirdly want to change them, be that one girl who makes everything okay again. We never do! It can at times feel like such a massive blow that you don't even know if you can get back up from it. It is gut-wrenching and, all these years later, I can remember how it felt to be used without realising it. I guess I was naive but when you are desperate for love and affection you don't see it like that.

I remember moulding myself to be the person they wanted. I would send the sexy photos where I didn't feel comfortable because they would tell me 'they were getting bored' and I was desperate for their attention, only to find they then never replied. I was so young, so inexperienced and so easily used because I wasn't looking for the person who fit me, I was constantly changing to fit around them. No doubt because this whole new Someone Likes You was brand-new territory I hadn't experienced before.

I can remember being 16, in an alleyway with a boy. (Remember, I'm the girl no fucker wanted.) I was desperate to be that person because it's what all the girls did, but I was petrified. He told me to give him a blow job and I said no. He tried to force me, and I said, 'Please don't, I don't want to.' He then called me a slut and a prick-tease as I tried to edge away. No man should treat a woman this way, but I didn't see that and felt like I was the person who was wrong. All I wanted was a kiss, I didn't know how to do anything else, and quite honestly I wasn't ready, but I was desperate to be that girl because I wanted to prove to myself I would push past that fear. Truth was, I couldn't, and I felt every single word flying out of his mouth when he verbally abused me as I escaped. That was the general experience I had of men, even at that age. I was shamed when I didn't do as they told me to. I was constantly under the illusion that I wasn't good enough and that the only good man I could rely on to treat me with respect was my dad.

I did find the good guy, I fucked it up for a moment or two but we did make it through. I know of women who get hurt repeatedly by the bad guy, but just keep going back for more, hoping this time it'll be different.

I imagine there are way too many women reading this right now knowing that deep down that is them. I can see how that happens; love is a powerful thing and it can lead you down paths you will wish you hadn't walked. You don't feel strong enough to live without them even though in actual fact you could be so much stronger if you told them to just fuck off. You just don't see how incredible you are without that person. I hope you find the strength to break free and understand there is a much better life for you out there.

I'm not in a perfect relationship because those notions are only for Hollywood big screens, but I have a choice to be who I am without Steve expecting me to be something else. The hardest part about that statement is that I am to some considered lucky to have a man like that and I shouldn't take him for granted. He's considered patient and amazing, while I'm just labelled lucky. Hang on! How is that even possible? Owning a vagina doesn't make me a second-class citizen; I don't need to check in with him to ask how I should be feeling. It's time you challenged that! I wish I had given myself this level of respect back then, when I was just desperate to be accepted. I really wish I had said no to the men who I just hoped would like me. They never deserved me, and I feel ashamed for allowing that to be a part of my life, even though it has taught me to be more resilient and confident about who I am. What a shitty way to learn.

Steve and I piss each other off frequently, and I will lose my shit sometimes if he even rolls near me in bed, but I couldn't be without him even for a second of my life. We have a strong relationship but that has come off the back of some of the most heartbreaking, soul-searching and difficult times, and I'm not stupid enough to think we don't have more of those times ahead. All good things take hard work and sometimes along the way we get our vaginas stuck in zippers to remind ourselves of the pain we have to go through to keep the romance alive.

-Laura's Life Lesson - - - - -

If you don't have a man in your life, allow me: know beyond all measure how incredible you are for caring for your kids, putting everyone first and never giving up. You are the gravity in the world of the lives around you. You won't always think it, but without you to steer that ship (the one that holds your kids and the house you live in), it would sink. May I also take this perfect opportunity to say congratulations on not settling for the shit relationship with the guy who doesn't make you happy. Well done for actually understanding you deserve more than whatever they have to offer, and, lastly, thank God for good dildos; they just never let you down.

> *'The guy we settle down with isn't*
> *necessarily going to be the person we*
> *want to die with. It's no one's fault; it's*
> *how life evolves and how our priorities*
> *change.'*

I think, as you get older, your relationship evolves and your tick lists change, and that's how things can begin to break down.

In your teens all you care about is getting pissed, losing your virginity and going steady with someone longer than a week while trying to dodge all sexually transmitted diseases. Your aim is to finish school with enough qualifications to start your own million-pound business and be the next Alan Sugar, and you genuinely believe it is that easy. You tell yourself you'll move out at 17 and find the love of your life by 18, because it's just so simple.

In your early twenties you find there are men who treat you like a jack hammer, repeatedly in and out of you like you're a DIY workout, some who expect sexual favours with nothing in return, and a whole lot of disappointment unless you're doing it yourself because actually these boys don't massively know what they're doing other than repeatedly shoving it in your hole, over and over. You drink, and drink. You wake up at midday and smell like an elephant just took a dump in your mouth because you went out last night and ended up in some random bed. You kind of navigate the shit boyfriends while wondering if you will ever find the person who isn't a total arse rag. That million-pound business looks a whole lot like an admin job that pays okay, but by the time you've paid for that rental flat and put petrol in your granddad's old Micra, you're skint as fuck, but it's okay because you're young, free and willing to suck anything that smells like Paco Rabanne and shows you some attention.

– The slut rant – – – – – – –

Before I move on to late twenties let's just have a quick chat about the idea a women sleeping around is considered slaggy ... Why is that?? So the man is called a hero, good in bed, a legend, with women falling at his feet on the assumption he's a demon in the sack, all because he stuffs his sausage into multiple McMuffins? Yet, when a woman navigates her sexual desire to sleep with whoever she chooses, she's deemed a slag, shit in bed, unable to hold down a man, she lacks respect for herself and isn't someone you'd like to take home to Mum? HOLD UP!! No, actually, we have the right as women, just as much as you do, to freely roam as many beds as we choose without the names and accusations. No, she isn't going to sleep with your husband, and while I'm sure Brian is a real killer between the sheets, a single woman enjoying her sex life doesn't make her a home-wrecker, no more than it does a man who doesn't want to settle down. Enjoy it without fear of those shitty looks and narrow-minded views, but for the love of fuck just regularly get checked for STDs.

Rant over.

In your late twenties you all of a sudden start to feel the tug of your womb screaming – give me a baby to birth. You are now looking at the managerial job that started out as someone's admin bitch in that office and you've been with this guy for two years and things are going well. You've bought the house, yes! You both managed to get the new cars, yes! Promotion, yes! Before you know it, you're married, yet the struggle is still real. The mortgage repayments are a bitch and you just about manage a two-week all-inclusive once a year in Turkey, but you don't care because you're happy. You have the baby, it might be that that process wasn't as straightforward as you hoped – IVF, adoption – but you made it and you're winging it into your thirties, feeling like you are fully fledged adults, but you still haven't got a fucking clue what you're meant to be doing.

Then you hit your thirties and it's so much fun; you have young children, it's exhausting and those days of long lie-ins and sex until noon are a distant memory. Actually, those fun moments where you would kiss, hug and hold each other daily are fizzling out a bit, too. Wow, the kids just take up so much time, and those holidays they kind of come every other year now courtesy of that fuck-off credit card because now you have to pay the arsehole prices that the travel companies put on during the school holidays. It's fun, right?? But like a massive drug binge, the beginnings of the comedown where you're still smiling but you're not sure if you're having fun any more is starting to set in. That promotion – you have to weigh up if you take it or step to one side because you've got kids to consider. Either way, it's a massive juggling act, one you never really feel you get to grips with. You hold his hand less, you don't want sex as much, you question what interests you have still, but you're both living life in the fast lane so you don't often have time to dissect that feeling.

You fall into your forties with more wrinkles than you had expected and twice as many pubic hairs. Those cute kids, they now have mouths on them and actually they don't often give you the respect you deserve because they think they know everything (and meanwhile you feel like an utter cunt for treating your own mum and dad like this in your teens). You know it's a rite of passage for your kids to be arseholes but you wonder if they will make it to adulthood. You get to a point where you actually stop and look at your husband and it feels like a mild, warm friendship, where you share a bed and very rarely show him your increasingly saggy tits – that passion is long gone. You miss the fun, you miss the freedom, but most of all you miss having the person who made you love life. The mortgage is still there and you're trying to decide if that job is right for you any more. Actually, what made you happy before doesn't give you the same burst of adrenaline. It's the same, it's unexciting and you've now been doing it for what feels like an eternity but how do you break free? When it's the safe comfort of what you are used to, it's reliable and it doesn't push you into unknown scary territory. You look back at what was important when you first started this journey and you realise something needs to change but you're not sure what, but that rut is old and tired.

I'll be honest, I could get into your fifties but then that's the menopause and I do believe that's a whole other book entirely. I'm also a way off from having the fun trials and tribulations of hot flushes, insomnia and crippling mood swings. Truly, though, I can't wait! You live your life meeting people, falling in and out of love, moving, learning and changing constantly with your surroundings and you are going to sometimes let go of people you never thought you'd lose – friends, husbands, partners, wives. Divorces will happen, separations, affairs, deception and pain, all because as you've grown so has your tick list of things you want and expect out of life. Life would be utterly boring if we never wished and hoped for more. The guy we settle down with isn't necessarily going to be the person we want to die with. It's no one's fault; it's how life evolves and how our priorities change. It's at this point I envisage Steve reading this chapter and going: 'Fuck, I've got another five years before the bitch is going to leave me.'

I think to survive every hurdle it's about being honest. Okay, so you aren't sexually attracted to him any more – talk, change it up, make the difference because if you love them enough, things are actually worth fighting for. Steve and I survived our separation by being honest. Which at times was painful, needing and expecting and then hearing every detail of what that person did during your time of singleness. I don't remember enjoying it much, but thank fuck we did it because it's without a doubt what helped us pull it through to the other side – somehow, and by the skin of our teeth. I live by the rule that honesty is the best policy, unless you forgot to flush that shit in the toilet and then you blame the kids.

> *'Deep below that need to care for a needy*
> *human, we were still those people who fell*
> *in love and had so much fun together ...*
> *I think it's healthy to take those moments*

*for each other. It isn't selfish; it's required
to still have a relationship worth living for
once your kids have grown up and fucked
off to live their own lives.'*

Steve and I aren't doing a particularly great job of being
the best version of ourselves and we often get to the
end of the day regretting something we have done, but
we are just trying our best. We miss time alone while
constantly feeling like we should be making more of the
time we have with our kids, and we feel the heavy guilt
that weighs us down for wishing we could get rid of them
for a night or two.

I remember Elliott was about 18 months old when
I first organised a night away in London, kid-free. Up
until that point I had felt like that we weren't husband
and wife any more; we were just parents. All we talked
about was him, how we loved him, what we needed to get
for him and our plans for the future. We just didn't talk
about us any more and I hadn't realised how much I had
missed that until I had stopped and truly taken stock of
how long a year and a half is when you just don't ask each
other how you are. Being his parent was so consuming I
didn't know how to be Laura with Steve any more.

That night away was so incredible because I realised, for the first time since becoming parents, that
we were still there. Deep below that need to care for a
needy human, we were still those people who fell in love

and had so much fun together. Even all these years later – now the parents of two demanding and wonderful children – I have not forgotten how that felt, how relieved I was that we hadn't completely lost each other.

I think it's healthy to take those moments for each other. It isn't selfish; it's required to still have a relationship worth living for once your kids have grown up and fucked off to live their own lives. Finding the babysitter isn't easy, it isn't always cheap, but, Jesus, just do it. Every so often find someone – a grandparent, an auntie, the teenage kid next door – to just sit in your house for a couple of hours so you can hold hands and remember all the reasons why you even wanted to have sex with this man to create these little spawns of Satan.

-Laura's Life Lesson - - - - -

This one is for the dads, a reminder of her worth. Her job, it never ends. Literally from the moment that baby screamed and took its first poo, she entered into the hardest job of her life. It will test every single inch of her patience, but it will bring her love on a level she never knew possible. This woman, who never gives up, at times feels tired, unloved and unworthy. Remind her why she is amazing. Be sure to tell her she's as beautiful as the day you met her. Remind her why she matters.

Arse brooms

I do believe that you could say that *at times* we live like pigs in shit. Mainly because I'm a lazy bitch and I can't say I care any more. I am tired from what life throws at me. I don't want to be that person who pretends she spends hours cleaning, when in actual fact I sit on my arse looking through Instagram, as my kids flick bogeys on the carpet and teabag the sofa (anyone who lacks the luxury of knowing exactly what this means – it's the nutsack smacking something. Yes, it is as delightful as you'd imagine. Yes, we invested in leather sofas for the wipe-clean option).

Don't tell me the job of housework is a woman's job – BITCH, PLEASE! You have hands, now grab the bleach and remember we share this home equally. We work hard in different ways and I'll be fucked if I have to be the only one to make this place look like less of a shithole all because 'my mum never showed me how to work a washing machine'. Let's not blame that shit on your mum – granted I have a few words for her letting you get away with it, but you're a big boy now. I think you can handle this responsibility.

The unfortunate fault in my genetics as a woman is that I didn't get the cleaning bug. You know the one where you stay up until midnight cleaning the bathroom. I admire those people, I really do, but I take no real pride in scrubbing skid marks out of a toilet when I could be watching a movie and falling asleep on the sofa.

Tradition has had it that the woman cooks and cleans, while the man works hard in the day to bring home the bacon. Well, we're kind of pretty far away from the post-war days where that was deemed acceptable and I really don't understand how a 'woman's work' isn't also considered hard and demanding. Just saying, try doing 40 loads of washing while shaking a small child off your leg as they go through the biting stage, then come back to me and say who gets it harder. God forbid you are a woman with a career too, because then all of a sudden that hard work of bringing home the bacon is shared! I believe in equality and any half-decent man who agrees with that notion also understands the fact the house isn't a woman's job, it's a job to be done together. You pay those bills? Well, guess what, it's time you got to those dishes too. We are now in a place where some women are earning more than their partners (about time) and working those five-days-a-week kinds of job where all of a sudden they have housework, childcare, social life and downtime to balance. You wonder why we get pissy when shit doesn't get done, because babes it's OURS to share. For example:

- Firstly, let's not sit there and pretend you can't hear me clanging around the kitchen like I'm catching flies with saucepans. All that noise is a request for you to come and help me.

- There aren't many things in life I like to label as a blue job. In fact, there is only one, and it's called emptying the bin. Yes, I will continue to shove stuff into it until the bin bag splits. Probably best you keep on top of that.

- We don't have the designer home. The sooner we both get over that the better.

- What the fuck is that on the carpet? Shit or chocolate? Either way, I don't want to smell it.

- I prefer to work on a 'let's put as many clothes in the washing machine as possible and hope the drum doesn't break under the strain' kind of basis. It works well. We've only replaced the washing machine four times.

- Do not step over that scaggy pair of pants on your side of the bed. I'd prefer not to touch them and you know that massive mound in the hall is our designated smelly rag pile.

- I'm tired, you're tired – let's just give ourselves the empty promise of doing the housework tomorrow so that we can watch Netflix.

* Every single time we have guests coming I will make you put the wash basket in the loft because it's operation shove and hide. It's important that people believe we have our shit in order.

* That toy box with the broken lid, you forget how utterly vile it is until someone is sat there, looking at it with slight disgust while wondering if they should accept that cup of tea you're offering.

* Can you smell that? It is old cheese? Is it a dead mouse? No, it's that apple he bought the kids four months ago but instead they stuffed it down the side of the sofa to slowly rot. Somehow he will be the one in the shit for this, not the kids.

* I have as much time to clean the car as I do to complete a 40,000-piece jigsaw puzzle; just tuck 'n' roll, and hope for the best. You shouldn't have to sit on pre-chewed gum, but if you do I apologise in advance.

* I am going to use your razor to shave my armpits and pubes. You will hate it but sadly it is something you need to get the fuck over.

* Clean the sheets when they start to smell like dead scrotums and ignore all smells leading to that point because trying to put the bedsheet back on is like trying to wrestle a hostile ghost.

* Let's get takeaway and leave it all out on the sides to ferment overnight so that the house looks and smells like a student just farted in our living room.

It's going to be alright, she says
with tears in her eyes, as she
stumbles around in the dark for
a while trying to find the light.

6

Why can't I love you?
Postnatal depression

> 'I had the loving husband, all the things
> we needed to have a happy little life, and
> yet here I was so very desperate, sad,
> lonely and scared.'

When the lights go out, it can happen fast. Like a steam train that just absolutely knocks the shit out of you when you least expect it. Everyone around you is quick to say that they don't understand why you feel sad, that you have no reason to be depressed. 'Look at all the positives!' Then there is my all-time fave: 'Why don't you go out for a walk and get some blue sky, green grass and fresh air.' Like, the fucking sky is going to snort your sadness out like a line of cocaine. I have never felt so lonely, and yet surrounded by so many people, as I did during this period of my life. Everyone wanted to help, yet all it seemed to do was remind me how sick I was and how far away from myself. I was sinking, fast, and not only was I sinking, but I was suffocating in the most petrifying way, because no professional was listening to my screams for help.

The only way I can describe my behaviour is: I went into hospital as normal to give birth to Elliott (as normal as I'll never be) and I left batshit crazy. It isn't like a slow-burning candle that melts into the ground; it is almost instant. Within 24 hours I begin to act strangely but when you've never experienced anything like it you just don't question it. This new sensation didn't feel good but was it just the side effect of having a baby? Like that 1 in 10 million chance of an adverse reaction to taking a paracetamol. I stopped eating, I didn't sleep, and I erratically went from feeling on top of the world to being so utterly depressed and in the depths of despair within hours of each other. My mood was all over the place, but I was desperately trying to tell myself it wasn't postnatal depression. I was in denial and I constantly blamed this tiny new person who seemed to be sucking the life out of me. How could something so small be so draining and demanding? It would seem I couldn't cope with that level of neediness, maybe because I'm that needy bitch on a daily basis and there is only so much room for drama queens. I wasn't living, I wasn't laughing, I wasn't enjoying, I was merely existing.

At times, suicide felt almost close to a sexual fantasy – 'All that sleep'; 'I would never hurt again'; 'This horrible feeling I can't shake, it would be gone'; 'I wouldn't have to live in this misery any more'. It was selfish, but that's because depression makes you a selfish person – you are totally consumed with yourself. I remember my mum saying to me at one point, 'Laura, you need to talk about something else. You're obsessed.' She was right; I was obsessed, because to a certain degree I couldn't actually believe I could be living with this endless level of misery. How could my brain switch from being that person who washed and ate food to 48 hours later feeling like a demented hag with no desire to hold her baby and who utterly hated the very existence of his little life? I wasn't the person forced into this; I was the person who wanted to be a mum from as far back as I could remember. I had the loving husband, all the things we needed to have a happy little life, and yet here I was so very desperate, sad, lonely and scared.

I felt like my postnatal depression with Elliott was the absolute worst. I was neurotic, I was at the doctor every other day asking what was wrong with him. He screamed all the time, colic is a total twat and being a first-time parent I was pretty sure he was just broken. 'Someone fix him or exchange him for a kid that sleeps more and makes noise less!' Sadly, though, there was no exchange policy going at the reception of my doctor's surgery. I had also been told selling babies on eBay was frowned upon, although it felt tempting at times to give it a try, because I would look at people without children and I'd wish to be them. 'Take me back to the old me who didn't have this responsibility!' My happily ever after really was acting like a total shitter.

Elliott was six weeks old when Steve made a panicked phone call from work to my dad, saying he needed to check up on me immediately because he was worried I would do something stupid. Dad arrived at my house to find me sat on the sofa holding my screaming baby and crying. I told him I couldn't do this any more. I admitted I had driven to the beach late one night – on one of my shifts to drive Elliott around in the car because it was the only way to shut him the fuck up – and contemplated walking into the water.

I wish I could say the visit to the doctor that day with my dad holding my hand was the saving grace in my life. Truth is, it wasn't, because they treated me like a small child. They had seen how many times I had visited the surgery in the last six weeks with my irrational behaviour, they had seen that I had begged a GP to give me sleeping tablets because I was waking in the early hours each night becoming violent, suffering the worst insomnia, and they labelled me overanxious and a timewaster. I was told on one occasion to get a grip, because I was one of many mothers, and yes it was hard, but this was what parenting was. (That totally helped my level of despair about how shit I saw being a mum as.) I wish I could say it was my local GP surgery who helped me heal, but the reality is they let me down massively. I was prescribed antidepressants, but within a couple of days I had convinced myself I didn't need them. I was on a high that day when I went back to the doctor and said, 'Actually, I'm having an adverse reaction to them.' The doctor said, 'I can see you're better! You clearly just needed to pull yourself together.'

Yeah, sure, because that's exactly how depression works, you bellend. 'Pull yourself together' ... that saying absolutely means jack-all when you're in your darkest moments. My doctor didn't see that emotional high as a problem even though just days before she had threatened to section me for saying I wanted to kill myself.

In the same appointment where I was basically patted on the back for 'pulling myself together' like a tantrumming toddler who had just calmed the fuck down, I was put on a muscle relaxant to help with my sleep, but also told they wouldn't refill my prescription. I was allowed two months, that was it. It was tough love on a monumental scale, and I felt like all I wanted to do was make the medical professionals proud of my recovery. How tragic! They ignorantly let me fester in the belief I had completely overreacted.

So, I managed to wean myself off the sleeping medication within that tiny two-month period, and I can't describe the level of anxiety it gave me. I would break a tablet in half, while sobbing that I was petrified it wouldn't work. I started acupuncture – it wasn't cheap, not even remotely, but I was desperate. I managed to keep that up for eight weeks before we just couldn't justify spending that kind of money. I felt well enough to make it alone, to try to find the good – even though my days were dark they now seemed light enough to manage.

I dragged my way through the first year not telling anyone outside of my family. It felt like a totally shameful thing to admit that I had been the mum who couldn't cope, because none of my other friends had these issues. The doctor had made me feel like a total failure; the shame and embarrassment of my friends knowing was just too much to bear. At the time I felt healed, but I wasn't; even when Elliott was four I wouldn't allow myself a whole day at home with him. I always found a reason to leave the house because I was terrified of how I'd feel at the end of that day. I always thought back to that day when Dad came round to my house when Elliott was a tiny baby, when I cried and told him I couldn't do it any more. I never wanted to go back there and so making sure I found reasons to leave the house daily seemed like my way to manage the problem.

> *'Nothing like knocking out another kid to remind you how unhinged you had been all along.'*

Nothing like knocking out another kid to remind you how unhinged you had been all along. Toby was born, and now I had a four-and-a-half-year-old *and* a newborn, and struggling with Elliott alone seemed like a trip to Narnia. The insomnia was back but it was different this time because I just didn't sleep. Nope, not a fucking wink. I counted sheep, channelled my inner Zen and snorted every kind of Holland and Barrett over-the-counter natural remedy that was meant to induce normal sleep – not a fucking thing.

I was unwashed, unhappy and at times completely out of control. I wasn't overanxious about Toby, I wasn't taking him to the doctor all the time with irrational worries, I just didn't give a fuck. Like, not even a little bit of a fuck. He felt like the biggest ball and chain around my neck, and I'd feel physically sick when people said how content he was when I held him. He seemed bonded to me, the person whose heartbeat he had listened to for the last nine months, who had shared a space within my body where I had protected him and done all the things I was meant to do to keep him healthy, and yet as soon as he was expelled from my body he seemed like the biggest mistake of my life.

I called the doctor. I told them in one of my highs that I needed sleeping tablets: that would fix everything. I gave up breastfeeding again just so I could take the tablets, even though I had been so desperate to make it work, but I just wanted to be better, be me again. At times I maxed out the dosage of the muscle relaxants. Previously one tablet would send me to la-la land within an hour: not this time! Three tablets down and I was still acting like that guy at a rave who took too much ecstasy. Still no sleep, and the doctors simply said, 'Then don't take as many', when I called erratically saying they made me feel even more depressed.

I was slowly going insane, and I needed someone to help me but no one was. My family were encouraging me by saying 'you seem better today!' They were attending doctor's appointments with me and speaking on my behalf. The doctor would listen to them and not truly look at me and the hole I was falling into. I don't blame my family. They were dealing with something so delicate and they were sure if they were positive it would in turn make me believe in myself. The problem was I was way beyond a pat on the back and a confidence boost. We went back and forth to my parents because I found I just couldn't cope. My mum would make bottles, she would help with night feeds and in all honesty keeping us all afloat, because Steve was hanging by a thread too.

He was beyond exhausted – he was so worried about me while trying to balance being a dad and working full-time.

The doctor once again ignored my pleas and I turned to acupuncture, except this time that didn't work either. It was £46 a time and we just didn't have the money, like not even close, to be able to keep that habit up. My last visit was when Toby was three weeks old, and I told the clinician who owned the practice I would be going to the doctor for antidepressants because I was at breaking point. She advised me of how toxic they are. That they are addictive and more often than not they make you worse.

I left paralysed with fear, out of money to burn and options to use. I thought, it'll be alright, I'll give it time and I imagine I'll feel better. Yeah, that didn't happen. I had been given a prescription of strong sleeping tablets, which were working: the new mum who should have been getting up with her baby through the night was taking a horse tranquiliser and hoping it made her sleep, which it did, and yet there were still times Steve would find me stumbling around the house, half a droopy tit hanging out of my top, mumbling that I needed to be up and I needed to help. He would usher me back to bed and tell me to rest, and my body fought me every single inch of the way to resist sleep.

I wasn't that mum who proudly sat there talking about how exhausted she was because her baby was up all night; I was the ashamed mum who tried not to enter into conversations about her son's sleeping pattern because truth was I didn't massively know. We needed help, and yet again we were being let down because no one would listen to ME, listen to me and stop telling me to focus on my baby.

> *'I wasn't bothered, though, because I was having a general anaesthetic, which meant I was going to sleep; and, fuck my life, having suffered with the worst case of insomnia, I literally couldn't fucking wait.'*

Now, this is a fun story. Newborn, shit! Postnatal anxiety, really shit! Postnatal depression, doubly shit! Gallbladder, you're joking right? Liver failure, someone get this bitch a seat on *Oprah*. She has a story to tell.

So, I was four weeks post-birth, finally managing to eat food without it tasting like cardboard, having lost all my baby weight and then some, a baby with colic, a child who fucking hated his baby brother and resorted to kicking and punching me at every opportunity because he also hated me and a school run to manage, when all of a sudden I was suffering with pain so horrific I thought that the alien that had burst out of the dude's chest in the film had crawled up my arse and was about to do the same.

I mean, fuck! I would finish the school run, get home, burst through the door and just about manage to get to the kitchen sink and projectile vomit. I was on such strong sleeping tablets I decided I had a stomach ulcer, I was medicated, the medication made my vomit glorious colours and, guess what, my life was shit but it would seem it was about to get shitter.

One Thursday evening when Toby was just under six weeks old I told Steve my piss was so bright if you turned a light off, it would glow. I had drunk nine pints of water, nothing was making a difference and I'm now 48 hours into highlighter piss, which is doing my anxiety no favours. Steve said, 'Laura, your eyes are yellow!' So, I casually call 111, 'Oh yeah, I'm pissing bright rainbows, shall I take a paracetamol?' They asked the usual of are you or have you been bleeding from your vagina heavily in the last two hours, to which I always wonder how the fuck that has anything to do with it?!? I answered no and they said, 'Laura, we need you to get to A&E now.' It was 10.30 at night and I had basically managed nine hours' sleep in twenty days. I was hanging. I arrived at the hospital to be told it was a five-hour wait. Fuck that! I went home, did the school run and decided I'd pop by the doctors at some point.

I was now back to eating nothing because whatever I put in my mouth seemed to react like an internal volcano about three hours later. I looked like hammered shit, and I felt like it too. I arrived at my doctors once again with my wonderful dad holding my hand, literally wondering how the fuck he manages to get into these situations with me. The doctor looked at me, hammered shit with a baby in tow, and said, 'I am calling the surgical unit now, I think you have gallstones.' This was the first time someone mentioned those words to me and now having had them, please take it from me when someone says I have gallstones and they hurt, they are playing it down because the actual description is something trying to tear your sternum out.

I rushed over to the hospital with a grumpy prick of a baby that cried, a dad who barely knew how to hold a baby that young and was no backup, Mum was at work (I could tell by the look on my dad's face he was just begging for Mum because she just knew how to deal with that shit), Steve was at work, a child at school ... Fuck, the kid at school! My sister collected Elliott, Dad held the screaming baby and the surgeons sent me for scans.

I remember lying, the silence of the room was deafening, the sonographer was saying nothing; she had already confirmed I had in fact got gallstones but she wasn't scanning that area any more. She was scanning my side, and then she left the room. She came back with another doctor.

'Laura, we don't want to worry you but we've found something on your liver. The lead consultant is going to look for me.'

No matter how many times you get told not to worry, you instantly go to holy shit stations. They both silently stood, looking: nothing. NOTHING! Jesus guys, throw the girl a fricking bone!!

'Laura, please try not to worry but you have three lesions on your liver and we now need to get the registrar in to look into this further.'

They left the room, and I was all of a sudden completely alone, and I said the words, 'Please God don't let me die.' I had toyed with death so many times over those initial weeks of having Toby but all of a sudden the true reality really did scare the shit out of me.

The registrar entered, he scanned me, the others looked on with faces that said, 'Shit, bitch, this is bad.' He once again said, 'Laura, please try not to worry but we will need to take you to another room because one of the three lesions is very big.' Fucking awesome! Just so you know, telling someone to not worry is a personal invite to worry.

I spent 25 minutes silently believing I was a 31-year-old new mum suffering with the worst postnatal depression and I'm about to be told I now have liver cancer to throw in too.

They put a drip in my hand, flushed dye through my system to confirm I didn't have anything other than three pieces of shiny liver. This bitch is gold plated! Who knew?!?!

Within two days of my hospital admission I was back in surgery having my gallbladder out, and all I could think was, 'Thank God I will now get help with the kids, I need to recover.' I was meant to be nervous as the trainee surgeon repeatedly stabbed my hand with a needle, saying, 'Oh, I'm sorry I didn't get the vein that time.' After seven attempts she kindly suggested she got someone else – YA THINK?!? I wasn't bothered, though, because I was having a general anaesthetic, which meant I was going to sleep; and, fuck my life, having suffered with the worst case of insomnia, I literally couldn't fucking wait. I kept it a secret that I had been taking sleeping tablets because I felt so ashamed, I was getting an overnight stay luxury of the NHS and I couldn't wait! Roll round the next day, one organ down, 12 puncture wounds from multiple medical professionals trying to get a vein and failing and I was on my way home. Completely gutted I wasn't actually at death's door because at least then I might actually get to stay in hospital longer. Turns out I had time to digest that thought and it didn't seem so bad after all.

'Laura, I promise you are going to be okay.'

Time sulked on in the slowest way possible, and these fucking kids really needed me, which was totally killing my buzz, only the buzz was the constant sound of intrusive thoughts about how much my life fucking sucked and how utterly lonely I felt. I'll never forget the day, Toby was 11 weeks old and it was the Friday Elliott finished school for half term. I was out for lunch with my sister and I said to her, 'He is fucking killing me, I hate that I have to bring him everywhere. He never behaves for me.' My sister peered down at this perfectly sleeping baby and looked at me: 'Mate, you alright?'

Toby woke up and did what most babies do: he cried and I said, 'SEE!! Exactly what I'm talking about!' I had totally had enough of him. Poor prick, he had done nothing wrong; it wasn't his fault.

I left the pub we'd had lunch at and felt so out of control I didn't know how I could survive another night in this utter misery. I knew I was so sick but I had no idea how to make it better. My family were worried, and I felt like that was yet another massive chain hanging around my neck. I needed to look happy for them because I couldn't bear them needing to fix me. I collected Elliott from school, got home and with a shaky hand I called my doctors. This time, I hadn't cried. Not once! Baby blues, nothing! I had been emotionally empty for 11 weeks, and I couldn't explain why but it had gone – happiness, emotion – and all I had was my little friend called misery.

That afternoon was the turning point because the doctor who spoke to me saved my life. He was different to all the other ones and for the first time my story was listened to. He actually listened to me, and he promised me it was going to be okay. I told him how petrified I was of antidepressants and how everyone told me I would be addicted to the sleeping tablets if I kept taking them.

He said, 'Laura, I promise you are going to be okay.'

And now I cried. I didn't even need to try, the tears just rolled endlessly down my cheek and off my chin. He was going to help me get better.

I don't think I stopped crying from that point onwards for months – it was like I was making up for lost time. I couldn't form words without the tight drag of my cheeks pulling either side of my face like I was trying to disguise my anguish with a smile. I guess it was a sign of my recovery, but fuck crying that much about everything, including my food being too hot, didn't feel much like recovering. It felt like shit because accompanying those tears were the hot-poker pangs of pain in my heart. I called my doctor way more than I should – the overanxious twat who had a new problem every day was back – but this time I was made to feel welcome. He soothed my fears as I promised him that one day I would call him without crying.

The shitter about antidepressants is there is a chance they will make you feel worse before they do their work and, because they're the equivalent of a snail in relation to getting things done, that can take a while. In my case, it was five weeks before I could feel the edge of its shit starting to lift, before I started to smile and actually feel it. Although it was fleeting, it was something to give me hope. Good things were happening and I was ever so slightly warming to my humans. They were kind of cute – I guess.

'Is this life just dicking with me? Or did I just belly laugh!?! And MEAN IT!?!'

I can't say my bond was instant with Toby. It took me such a long time to see past the fact all I did was wipe his shitty arse while trying to feed the mouth of another human being who was equally as demanding. It was slow, but I did start to appreciate his smiles and his giggles.

The truth was he got all the love he needed from Steve. Steve was the most amazing pillar of support to us all. Looking back, I have no idea how he managed to keep us all alive, absorbing all of my verbal shit that flowed daily, where I overanalysed everything, and somehow still managed to be a relatively well put-together human being. As I learnt to walk again, he just slowly walked at my pace, showing me how to be the mum Toby and Elliott deserved. This is what having the stability of a confident person in my life meant. Every single time I stumbled he just instinctively caught me, dusted me off and got me back on my feet again. He was the reason I never gave up – not the kids, not our life, not my family – just Steve, sometimes mainly out of guilt but also because I knew I couldn't break his heart and step off the edge.

I never got better for me. I think there were periods of time where I didn't feel worthy enough to get better for me, but I always knew I needed to do it for him. I couldn't leave him to be the single widowed dad, and so we powered on through together. It sounds romantic and wonderful, which I guess it is, because I know many women don't have the luxury of a supportive partner, but in actual fact the reality is dirty, ugly, sad and distressing to watch. To watch a full-grown man restrain his wife in bed in the middle of the night as she spat in his face and said she was going to get a knife to end it all isn't the beautiful part of having someone help you get better. Having a husband arrive home to find his children crying and a wife sitting on the floor of the kitchen looking at the cupboards, who should have eaten her lunch and drunk a couple of glasses of water but kind of forgot the basic human survival instinct of how that shit keeps you alive. This isn't the happy ending we all hope for, but it is the reality.

While I can't remember exactly when it happened, I know that when my bond came back with Elliott and I found my love for Toby it was nothing short of wonderful. I would hug Elliott if he fell over and I'd feel that thing you do as a mum, that urgency to take the pain away for them coming back, and I felt proud to ache like that again. I started taking photos of Toby and recording him giggle – I hadn't bothered up until that point, but now I was finally able to start making memories with them, long overdue memories.

Have you ever tried so hard to force something for so long that when it finally does start to fall into place you question if the feeling you have is real? Like, is this life just dicking with me? Or did I just belly laugh!?! And MEAN IT!?! All this time, wandering around in the dark, I had no idea that these things that had turned my life upside down would go on to be my biggest inspiration to just be me and accept every single inch of its imperfection.

> *'No matter how hard you might avoid it, how fast you try to run from it or refuse the responsibility of it, eventually the love for your children catches up with you. It hits so you so hard that it leaves you with a permanent ache in your heart and a smile on your face.'*

My inspiration will always be Steve, because he dragged me through, single-handedly, with no knowledge of how depression works. It truly was the blind leading the blind. Through that all, though, my biggest thanks will always go to my boys, Elliott and Toby. It has been the determination of both Steve and me that forced me to get better – for them, for us. Steve could see the potential I had to be the best mum to them and he never gave up pushing me up that steep hill, and although having them brought on two of the most horrific mental breakdowns I have ever experienced, truth is I'd do it all over again for them. No matter how hard you might avoid it, how fast you try to run from it or refuse the responsibility of it, eventually the love for your children catches up with you. It hits so you so hard that it leaves you with a permanent ache in your heart and a smile on your face.

I was blessed with the most loving family – they hurt to see me so sick – and my friends, who silently weathered the storm with me. They say it takes a village and I've been incredibly lucky with the one I've chosen to live in. My village – Steve, Mum, Dad, Elliott, Toby, Emma, John, Dave, Lucie, Lisa, Lyndsey, Vicky – were always standing by my side, sometimes just to make me smile, or to remind me I can do this, and they will never understand how those small moments helped me to keep going. They hadn't gone through what I had and never really understood what I was going through, but they still loved me even though I didn't often feel worthy of that love.

Having someone listen, something I had never really had in my whole experience with mental health, was the turning point in my life; it was the catalyst that started my journey to getting better. The antidepressants and sleeping tablets were the aids I needed to feel like I was actually walking and not drowning. But actually the main thing that got me through was reading positive stories of people suffering with postnatal depression and who were taking the same drugs as me and were making it. I knew I couldn't mentally cope with the horror stories; my anxiety at that time caused me physical pain every single day and I knew I wasn't strong enough for that. So

I googled to find the good stories, the uplifting ones, and there were hundreds! It let me believe enough that one day I would be that person: coping, happy and stable.

So when the day came where I felt ready, I gave back to that forum what so many other women had given to me, even though they hadn't even realised at the time. I gave them a little hope by talking about my journey and how far I had come and how I had hoped to just help one person with my positive story. I was far from fixed but I was slowly gluing myself back together enough to be open and honest. This is the post I wrote all those years ago. I was still in the thick of it but it felt good to be in a place positive enough to write the words:

Hello all you wonderful Mummies, Daddies and everyone in between,

Please excuse my inability to used shortened phrases, I'm new to this forum game (be kind). I wanted to share my story to hopefully help those struggling and needing something to keep them going. I am the proud mother to 2 beautiful little boys, one is 5 and the other is 7 months. I have wanted to be a mum my whole life so when I fell pregnant with my eldest son at 26 I was over the moon, I couldn't wait to meet him, to hold him, to love him ... then he arrived!!! I wanted to still want all those things but I found myself staring out of my car window looking at all the people who didn't have children just wishing I was them. At 6 weeks I came crashing down, I was almost sectioned and put on antidepressants and allowed home on the promise I would be cared for by my father (who had luckily just retired) during the day and my husband in the evening. I couldn't get on [with] the antidepressants but came off them within a week feeling positive that acupuncture would get me through it, and it did. Although the first year was a real struggle, I got through it and slowly but surely my bond grew and my son was the centre of my earth, my absolute everything.

The whole experience left its scars and I felt petrified to have another child, as did my husband having witnessed what I had been through. We finally decided to try for another child and my gorgeous little boy arrived August 2015. He was so perfect, but sadly PND hit me again but this time much harder than before. I found myself once again looking out of my car window wishing I was anyone but me. I felt I couldn't go on and remember sobbing to my husband that I didn't think I could ever love him like I loved my eldest. It was my darkest time and this time the natural route didn't work. I finally decided to go onto antidepressants and they made me feel worse! I thought this was my life for ever, I had forgotten who I was, why I was even existing. I stuck with it, I tried my hardest to work through it each day telling myself I had to carry on. Thank god I did! My dose of Citalopram was increased to 20mg and with a positive twist I had next to no side effects like I had when I originally started them. I fast forward to now and I am me again. I love both my boys to the end of the universe and back again. I lost myself in a sea of deep depression and felt totally hopeless but a lot of what got me through was going on forums like this reading stories of mums saying just stick with it, it will be worth it. I am now that mum telling anyone struggling right now to keep with it because it will be okay. Listen to your body, be kind to yourself and most of all talk!

I was so sad to hear on the news recently how many women suffer with PND in silence. It is nothing to be ashamed of! We have grown a human being, given birth and [are] expected to hit the ground running. I have had the support of amazing family who have dragged [me] through those tough days and I am so thankful for them. Whether it be family or these forums that help just know you aren't alone and us mums have to stick together. I hope this helps just one mum out there struggling with either making the decision to go on antidepressants or desperately trying to deny they have it, I have been both of those people and it is heartbreaking. xXxXx

As a direct result of being so open on that forum, a woman who I'll call Emily, who was suffering much like I had, saw my post and messaged me. It was wonderful, because for the first time I actually had someone who got it. We both felt less alone, all because I had been brave enough to speak up to a group of strangers and tell them how my life got shit for a while. We chatted, sometimes daily, and the main subject was always centred around depression and how incredibly lonely it felt to be that mum utterly hating life. I wish now that I had found her sooner. I was five years into my journey as a parent, I was the newly confident mum of two who was heavily dependent on medication to keep her upright, but I was still here!! Why couldn't I have spoken up all those years ago? Been painfully honest? Because I realise now that I would have found out that I wasn't actually as alone as I thought.

We became friends on Facebook and to this day we keep in touch. We've never met but she was so important in my recovery. I am so thankful for her. She helped me in so many ways without even realising it. She got it! No one else around me did, and while I was considered the 'fixed' one as she was still working hard to get through the depths of depression, I was far from being the best version of myself. The wonder was we were effectively two strangers helping each other through something unknown and scary with a little love, understanding and kindness.

-Laura's Life Lesson - - - - -

Some days it's about knowing that even when the storm is blowing so hard and you aren't sure if you can hold out for the calm, remember you are so much stronger than you realise. Dig those heels in, throw your arms around yourself, close your eyes tightly and repeat the words 'You can do this. You will get through this.' Make that storm your bitch and believe you can ride your way out of its fury and fear with pride and strength. You got this, Mumma, you got this.

'I believe now that we all owe ourselves the full recovery.'

Steve and I made a choice to not have any more children. It was evident this journey I dipped back into wasn't ever going to get better, and actually who was that fair to? The boys? Steve? Or more importantly, me? So, when the kids say, 'Mummy, do you have a baby in there?' I can confidently reply with, 'No, sweetheart. Mummy loves carbs and Daddy got so scared she would go fucking mental again that he had his balls sliced open just to make sure he can't plant another demon seed inside my uterus.'

It has been at times a bitter tablet to swallow because instinctively my body tells me it'll be different next time, even though I know it won't! The female body is just mental. It will push you to the point of death and you'll still come back begging for more! They say you know when you're done, when you have absolutely had enough of pregnancy, babies and toddlers, and I guess I am, but more on a technicality because I have to continually remind myself that I don't do having babies very well.

Even now when I see newborns I can think back to being that mum and I find myself feeling physically sick. The thoughts, feelings and emotions are still there, because I can remember even down to smells how I felt as a person during that time. It didn't feel that way after I had Elliott, but it has stayed since having Toby. I border on feeling panicked when I hear a new baby cry because it can sometimes take me back to those days where I was the one owning the baby. I love to support women in these early days, I cook meals and take them round, even if I don't know them that well, because I have this overwhelming need to care for those mothers in the hope they don't suffer like I did. I am unsure what I think that cooked meal will do – fish pie isn't pioneering as a miracle cure to stop depression – but I feel this need to just DO something!

The funny thing with postnatal depression is that no matter how many times you visit its door, you stay in denial – mainly because you realise the moment you accept it's happening you then see the very long road to recovery, one I think I'm still on. Do we ever truly heal from that trauma, or do we just accept it and put a plaster over it and move on? I think we are all pretty terrible at taking those additional steps to really address issues, mainly because once we are partly better the pain is so much easier to manage and so we just keep on going, believing that all the time we can manage that thing we carry around with us we don't need to get any more help. I believe now that we all owe ourselves the full recovery. It's so scary, new, unknown and we have no idea where it will end, but we deserve to finish the chapters in books that we've left unwritten, the bit where we say, yes, this happened, no, it wasn't okay, and, yes, I am now officially strong enough to look you in the eye and say I am now truly, completely healed. I will carry you with me for the rest of my life, but I will no longer let your pain define my future.

knowing when and how to get help

- Babes, the moment you say I'll wake up in the morning and feel better but you're on day 36 of saying that same shit, might be time to talk.
- When someone asks, 'What have you got to be depressed about?', remind them their sheer ignorance alone is enough to make anyone shed a tear.
- There is no hard and fast rule to recovery. I'm sure Betty did manage to recover from postnatal depression in four days, but chances are she had baby blues and felt low. Let's not get that confused.
- When you go to the doctor and they spout some shit about take a look on this website if you tick more than three boxes with postnatal depression come back and see me (shit you not, I was told that), reply with: 'Shove that website up your arse and how about you help me now.'
- Don't be ashamed. Find that person who likes to listen. We all have that person and sometimes they're a lot closer than you think.

* Admitting it isn't a weakness. There is always strength found in getting help.
* Social services do not take babies and children away from women who have depression. Don't feel scared that by asking for medical help you will be judged.
* Not everyone will get it – not everyone matters. It's that simple!
* Trust your gut and when it says 'you gone crazy, bitch', just know it's time to owe yourself the honour of fixing what is broken.
* Don't take no for an answer. Medical staff know a lot of shit, but they don't know you. If you aren't happy with what one is saying, ask to speak to another.
* Don't sacrifice your own happiness for the benefit of others. Your life is too precious to be wasted trying to live up to the expectation of someone else.
* There will be good days, then there will be bad days. That, my friend, is what you call recovery and as you slowly recover so the bad days will begin to fade.
* Taking one step back isn't failing; it's living.
* Babies cry, we get pissed off, but when you think that cry is enough to make you headbutt a wall, it's usually the time to just check in with someone and verbalise that thought process.

❋ Not bonding with your baby isn't a sign of being a bad mum; it's a sign that your train decided to reroute and it's taking a minute longer than some to arrive at the destination.

❋ On the days when you feel like you can't cope, just don't! Find kindness for yourself, and don't let those 24 hours define the next one.

❋ You feel like the tunnel with the light might have relocated because it's pitch-black in here and some fucker forgot the torch. Listen to my voice – KEEP WALKING, the tunnel is there and the light is coming.

Dear Toby,

My one wish? To go back to the moment you were born and do it again. Why? Because maybe next time I'll love you sooner; maybe next time I'll remember these moments better. The reality is I can't go back and that is one of the biggest regrets I will have to live with. The saddest part: I have no real memory of our time together when you were very little! Because like a massive black hole, my memory of your life back then is gone; it's faded into a life I didn't live, and I'm sorry. All I ever wanted was you, but I got so sick I couldn't be the mum you needed. So, some pretty incredible people helped me get better while making sure you knew what love felt like, because I lost my way for a while.

I want you to know that I broke into a million pieces and glued myself back together differently with you by my side, and as a result Knee Deep In Life was born. From my heartbreak I found humour, from my troubled past I wanted to see people laugh, but this was what I always promised to be – honest.

So here is my reality. I am that mum who fell so hard she forgot what laughing was and knew how it felt to cry so much her eyes ran dry. I'm that mum who sometimes still needs to be told I'm a good mum because I feel I've failed again, but I know I've not.

Those days are designed to make the good ones look fucking awesome.

This message is who I am: imperfect and yet always trying my best to be better. I needed to share this, Toby, for those mums who believe they aren't ever going to love their baby, too. I need them to see that they aren't alone, and that while we never forget the pain, the love we find for our children is something worth waiting for, worth fighting for.

Thanks to you (and Elliott), I am here today, hop, skipping and jumping through life. But I'll be forever grateful to the people who made sure you learnt love beyond measure, and who captured the photos I couldn't.

You are the person who came into my life at the right moment and showed me how to share, love harder and work for the things I desperately wanted. Thank you for being that person to me, and, even though you don't realise it, I will always owe so many of the wonderful things that happened in my life to being a mother.

Mummy x

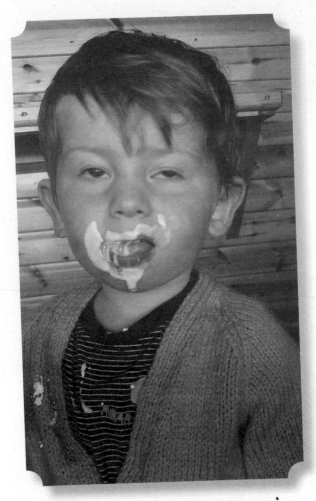

I love it when you scream in
my face about as much as I love
infected piles and here you are,
yet again, screaming like a
prick for no reason in public,
making me look like a shit
mum.

7

When will you wipe your own arse?

Here's to twatty toddlers

This is where I describe perfectly our lives as parents with a toddler. It's a cute one, so be ready for it ... I'm going to paint you the most incredibly beautiful scene that it's going to warm your heart.

Christmas is a very special time of the year for us –
we do it in a big way! I mean huge. From making cookies
to wearing matching PJs, we are those self-righteous
pricks who plague social media with the *almost* perfect
family photo, only someone is always crying and you
can guarantee Steve will blink every single time the
flash goes off. It is without a doubt my most favourite
time of the year.

Anyway, when Elliott was almost three, about three
weeks before Christmas, on a wonderful crisp day, Steve
took the day off so we could do lots of festive things
together. We went to the Winchester Christmas Market.
We went to Costa and ordered hot chocolate that tasted
like Santa's nutsack (and that shit isn't cheap). We
laughed and we played with Elliott. And, for the first time
since becoming parents, I actually felt like this was going
to be the Christmas where he truly got it! Like, holy fuck
the magic was finally going to arrive, and I couldn't wait.

And, because I could feel the magic, and because
being gutty pricks who ordered Santa's sack with a
cherry on top wasn't enough, we then chose to go to
the local Sprinkles, an ice cream parlour, where we
captured this tiny little person eating and being covered
in an abundance of ice cream! Oh my God, his little face
was adorable.

We left the shop holding his tiny little hand and
telling each other what a wonderful day it had been.

Elliott then asked us to do 1, 2, 3 swing and we happily obliged. Why not? Give the cute kid what he wanted. And, as he squealed with excitement, 'HIGHER MUMMY, HIGHER DADDY!', we swung him up even higher. As he hit six foot one in the air, Steve lost his grip. Oh shit. And like some kind of broken pendulum in slow motion, I saw Elliott begin to swing around in my direction. Oh fuck. Then I lost my grip (yeah, it's about to get bad). Like something out of *Kill Bill* (no swords were involved), I watched him gloriously fly through the air, face plummeting towards the concrete, and there was nothing we could do!

He hit the ground so hard that I believe my heart dropped out of my arsehole in that very moment.

As he lay there, completely lifeless, I thought, 'Fuck! That's ruined Christmas.' Steve, the least helpful person in a crisis, ran in the opposite direction, as I collected our tiny human up from the floor to find blood pumping out of his face like a water sprinkler. I'm not sure when Steve returned – I'll be honest, I'd started to wonder if he had full on Forrest Gumped out of our lives never to be seen again – but apparently he needed to debrief himself about why and how he had let go first. (*I've never let him forget that one.*)

Anyway, we managed to drive our broken, screaming, bloodied baby boy to the local hospital, Steve screaming, 'NNNEEE NNNAAAARRRRRR NNNEEE NNNAAAAA

RRRRRR YOU FUCKING WANKERS MMMOOVVVEEEE OUT THE FUCKING WAY. I WILL KILL YOU TRAFFIC LIGHTS, I WILL KILL YOU. AAAAHHHHHHH THIS IS ALL MY FAULT.'

In hindsight we probably should have called an ambulance, because any adult who openly says the words 'NNNEEEEE NNNAAARRRR' operating a vehicle is probably considered unhinged.

We arrived at the hospital and fitted into a scene out of *28 Days Later*. I ran up to reception: 'HELP!! MY SON, HE HE HE ... WE BROKE HIM!! PLEASE FOR THE LOVE OF GOD SOMEONE HELP US!' (Up until this point I had done such a good job of keeping it together.)

How did it end? I'll sing you a fitting Christmas song: 'On the tenth day of Christmas my true love gave to me, 1 broken nose, 2 parents crying, 3 broken teeth, 4 facial wounds, 5 nurses rushing, 6 pints of blood a-pumping (totally over-exaggerating), 7 hours of anguish, 8 bruises rising, 9 cuts and wounds, 10 extra gifts, and no fucking partridge in a pear tree.'

So, you know, that's life with a toddler.

'They just love you so much they never want to be apart from you, and there are just times when you wish you did a slightly shitter job of being a mum so that they didn't want this extra time with you of an evening.'

To be in ownership of a toddler it is important to remember the following: they are going to ask you 'why?' repeatedly, and no matter your answer they will continue to delve deeper into the reasoning behind your answer. Stay strong, because if I have to be honest this phase lasts approximately an arsehole period of time. It is cute to hear when you aren't in ownership of the child saying it, but they just don't shut the fuck up. I know I am not meant to say that because hearing your children call your name and ask you questions is precious, but it is also fucking mind-numbing:

'Mummy, why is this apple green?'

'Because that's the colour of apples.'

'Why?'

'Because the tree grew it that way?'

'Why?'

'Because that is the type of apple.'

'Why?'

'Because ... God made them green.'

'Why?'

'I don't know. He likes green.'

'Why?'

'I don't know.'

'Why don't you know?'

I am not even fucking kidding that you do that for two days straight. And tell me you aren't contemplating drop-kicking them into next week, because not only do they talk a shitload, but they also get night terrors. So you're there with your swinging sisters hanging out of your PJ top, patting what you think is their head but is in fact their arse in the dark, just hoping they go back to sleep because you're so fucking exhausted not just from all the questions but also their overwhelming need to try to detach themselves from you in public, throwing tantrums, and you having to tell them to stop putting their fingers up their bums because they've all of a sudden found a new fascinating hole to play with.

Don't worry, though, because then you have to navigate public spaces with a cute person who says 'cock' instead of clock, or 'dick' instead of stick, and somehow my child, for around six months, said sex shop instead of ketchup. It is hilarious until you're faced with another parent who no longer invites old Cussy Cuthbert round for dinner because he is now passing on his words of wisdom to her kids.

They wake up at the crack of dawn and you dare to contemplate that mid-afternoon nap, just for a little peace and quiet, only to find you have a mini raver until the late evening because you know you should drop that nap but you're not emotionally ready for dealing with a moody bastard from the afternoon onwards. They will throw their food on the floor just because they don't want it any more. And sometimes live off the same diet as a field mouse, picking up old crumbs from the floor while turning down the freshly made sandwich. The pearly gates of bedtime are within reach and you inwardly fist pump as you see the pyjamas being cracked out and the bedtime story being chosen – you made it through another day and no one died. Just as you believe you have reached the final countdown and you walk away, you hear the words 'Drink?', and so it begins, the untimely demise of your evening where you would sit on the sofa and do nothing, because that kid has a bigger tick list than Mariah Carey. They just love you so much they never want to be apart from you, and there are just times when you wish you did a slightly shitter job of being a mum so that they didn't want this extra time with you of an evening.

-Laura's Life Lesson - - - - -

When all else fails and you've absolutely had a gutful, give them McDonald's for dinner and let them play on the tablet until bedtime. Truly, they are living their best life on the days when you feel like you are totally failing. Let them have the shit most parents judge us for because the most important thing you can ever achieve in a day is keeping them alive. If you manage that, by whatever means possible, then you, my friend, are winning.

> *'They will draw on the walls, and they will laugh uncontrollably at their own farts and they will always absolutely love you no matter your mood, no matter what you have done.'*

I think my main hope of raising my children is that they aren't the shitter and spitter at the preschool gates, where the other kids start to cry when yours enters the room and mums avoid you like the plague. Don't even try to tell me you don't know that kid, because the reality is at some point or another all of our children will be that shitter and spitter. Whether it be at home or when you're out. I have wrestled and karate chopped irate shitbags into car seats as they've created merry fucking hell in the middle of a supermarket and had to drive them home ugly girl crying as they've continued to try to summon the fucking devil with their deep throaty moans of absolute rage because you wouldn't buy them the £40 remote control car.

I have also been that mother who has been called into preschool to ask if I am managing okay because, I quote, 'Elliott drew a lovely picture of you in chalk in the garden drinking from a bottle of wine. With no glass. He said you like to do that at breakfast …' Of course he fucking did!! How do you even remotely try to explain that situation when you're repeatedly told by medical experts that it's fucking impossible for a three-year-old to lie?? While I can admit to hitting some incredibly hard times, none of them included knocking back a bottle of Pinot Gris while pouring milk on his cornflakes at 7am.

Although it is a lot like watching a slow-motion car crash continually happening, day in, day out, there is something very special about hearing them call your name (unless it is repeatedly, and then you can assume the same process of drop-kicking them). It is those moments that make the awful early days, the sleepless nights, and crying, and constant BO smell because you never shower, all worth it. You feel their little hand reach up into yours, all warm, and then in a fleeting moment you look down at them and really see how tiny they are, how little they know about life, and all the things they are yet to learn. I would say that although this stage is so challenging it is my favourite.

They will draw on the walls, they will laugh uncontrollably at their own farts and they will always absolutely love you no matter your mood, no matter what you have done. They just love you in a way that truly shows, mainly because now they can actually say it. Which only makes you feel worse when you have lost your shit at them.

I used to look at the mums in the supermarket who carried on with their shopping as their kid literally almost coughed out a tonsil from screaming so much and I used to think what a shit mum they were. I didn't see the wrestle into the car seat, the slaps, kicks and scratches as she tried to then put them in the trolley, I never once thought about the fact she had no choice but to do that shop because she had nothing left in the house and I didn't think about the fact she actually wasn't asking for it. Not once was she hoping to walk around the shops being utterly humiliated by her child who, no matter what, was on a quest to totally ruin her life – maybe because they're hungry? Maybe because they're bored? Maybe just because they're toddlers and they're basically allowed to get pissed off over everything.

I wish I hadn't been that person, because I only added to her bullshit. And yes we all know the mums who scream at their kids and drag them down the high street, sobbing, yanking at their arm like it's about to be ripped off, and we all want to pick that child up and hug them. This woman in the supermarket – that isn't her. She isn't neglectful, she isn't cruel, she isn't swearing at the child; she's just trying to get home, where she will no doubt cry.

I have been that mum on so many occasions. More so with Toby, who I swear to God winds himself up as I go to walk into the shop knowing he will probably wait until I have at least half a trolley full before he gets pissed off and decides he wants to leave immediately, at which time I am then left with the decision of abandoning everything I have just spent 20 minutes collecting, or battening down the hatches and trucking on knowing he will be a total bellend for the entirety of that visit, and I am now that mum who is given the shitty looks for not controlling my child. Trying to control a toddler is like trying to take a drunk alligator for a walk. There is a strong chance they are going to attempt to walk out into the road on multiple occasions to try to scare the shit out of you and it's highly likely they will probably bite you, just coz!

They go through that phase, don't they, where they bite you and when you tell them off, they laugh. I have been told it's because children of this age are unable to understand the different emotions for each situation. I sometimes think it's because they're arseholes. In fact, when you have had an absolute gutful it is sometimes nice to think they are arseholes and not just going through a developmental change that involves being devoid of all emotions.

I can sit here and say that when my children have satanically laughed in my face as I've tried to discipline them, I've never lost my shit so badly that glass could shatter (because that isn't the correct way to parent small children finding their way), but when I am hanging by a thread and they choose to obnoxiously smile, it truly is my Achilles heel. I really can't cope with those moments and I know I should just walk away, be the adult in the situation, but I'm unsure if you're aware but they just follow you. Yeah, and they don't listen when you say go away! They just keep on coming, like a bad smell.

I know I'm not selling this period of time – it basically sounds more horrific than childbirth – but I think if there was any age I would like to last longer, it's this one. I'm not sure if it's because I like to torture myself for no good reason, but toddlers are a lot of fun, and they don't have outside influences getting in the way. It's not about the friends in school they've met. They want to be cuddled, they love to be kissed and they just enjoy your company regardless of whether you want to entertain them or not. While this age is wonderful, it is full on. You can't even leave the room to fart without them managing to find your sanitary towels in your handbag and sticking them all over the sofa (yes, that actually happened to me), even though you've told them enough times to stop fucking doing it. You aren't getting it wrong just because they are screaming, crying or not able to share; they're just being the most highly strung people you'll ever meet.

Would it be easier if we had help? I mean, hired help who live in, do all the exhausting night-time visits to and from their bedroom, with another child often sharing the parental double bed that was tight enough for two and is now busting at the seams? Of course, but I think in my utter madness this life is kind of what I signed up for – the chaos, the fact I am watched when I wipe my own arse and quite often look like I have yesterday's make-up on (and that's probably because I have!).

I am not criticising those who choose to have that help – in many circles you are considered weird if you don't have a nanny – but for me being a mum isn't about clocking off for lunches, massages, just because I've had a fucking gutful; it is in sickness and in health, through the rough and the smooth. I want to celebrate the tiny successes because I have seen the unbelievable amount of work it took to get to that point. I don't want to miss the tantrums, because they make me a better person in many respects. They make me more resilient to deal with the shit life throws at you.

I think because I missed out on so much of their baby days, I felt like I was owing these moments where I would scoop them up when they fell over and hug them until those tears ran dry. I want to be the person they run to, I want to be their everything, and while there are times when in actual fact Steve is, or my parents are, or my sister is the cool auntie, I am just so thankful that for the most part I am just there. Doing the shit mundane stuff that we all wish we didn't have to, because when these kids are older they will remember it: the arse wiping, plaster yielding, kissing, hugging, loving mum who was just there through thick and thin, who only ever passed them over to others when I needed my top lip waxing or on the very rare night off where I got to let my hair down and be me. I have been given the luxury of not having to work full-time, and for the most part been at home with my children. The career women are always judged for the level of childcare they have to use but honestly if I had been in a position where I did have the demanding full-time job and I had the option of a nanny to care for my children one on one, I'd take it. My point is, for all the moments I can be there I will be, because it's a time we find so long, hard and tiring, but all the same it's over so fast.

We will always wish for the easier life but truth be told, this long, drawn-out stage where they are trying to develop their speech, learning when not to throw a shit fit and still trying to sleep through the night is where I always wanted to be. It is perfectly acceptable to wish it away; there have been days, added together making weeks or maybe months, in my mothering life where I have wished for another day. But it still comes back to the same thing. You haven't gone anywhere, so deep down somewhere within your soul you must love it just enough to make it work, even through the tough bits.

I have reached a point now where those toddler days are gone; they are never coming back for me and I will miss them. The trying to work out whatever the fuck it is they're trying to say, listening to the obnoxiously loud way they eat food that weirdly doesn't make you want to turn into the Incredible Hulk. They are all yours and you choose to surround them with all the things that make them happy. It's rewarding because you can actually have a conversation, albeit in broken English, and you can see the fruits of your labour paying off. This kid is pretty alright actually.

Toddler truths

- They can be pricks. Let's not sugar-coat this with a deep-rooted explanation, sometimes it just feels good to call them a prick. Simple.
- Somehow they think it's totally acceptable to start the day at 4.30am, every day. No matter their bedtime. It's a shit time of the day to be awake. I hear you.
- They enjoy opening public toilet doors as you're halfway through changing your tampon, for 70-year-old Sheila to catch a glimpse of your hairy snatch.
- You will know in detail each episode of *Mr Tumble* and you will want to pull your toenails out with your teeth, but honestly it's the only thing that will keep the little bastard quiet for five minutes.
- Sticky hands. Everywhere. How? Why? I just fucking washed their hands!! How are there hand prints on my walls that look like something out of *The Blair Witch Project*??
- Their little hand holding yours as you walk down the road is precious because in that moment you realise: to them, you are their entire world.
- They enjoy walking away from you for no reason other than to test every single nerve you have in

your body. It's like a sequel to *Catch Me If You Can* except there are no cameras, and no other fucker trying to keep this walking thing in check.

✳ They will throw their food and refuse to eat it mainly because they hope in time they will break you and that biscuit on the side will be theirs to eat instead.

✳ I personally love it when they copy your sweet nothings. Such as 'you fucking wanker' as you suffer an outburst of road rage only to hear the small person in the back repeatedly say the word wanker for 50 minutes.

✳ You will check on them in their sleep and somehow that tiny moment of seeing them so peaceful will make you burst with love for them. That sleepy head moment wipes the slate clean for all the times they are total arseholes.

✳ They hate having their arse wiped, face washed and teeth brushed. It isn't fun but I believe that is why sometimes you can buy wine on special offer in the Co-op.

✳ Hearing them say 'I love you'. Yup, that little sentence alone is why we continually go back for more while suffering all of the above.

Dear Elliott,

My little man, you've been my shadow for nine years and I've loved every single moment, apart from when you've screamed in public and I've wished we could afford a nanny. You showed me the ropes, you taught me endless patience, unwavering love, how to multitask and how important it is sometimes to just walk away and count to ten.

One day you're going to be a grown-up and you're going to read this, so I'm going to say to adult you, I'm sorry! For everything! For losing my shit, wishing for your bedtime, and for being that mum who got her rack out over the internet and being no doubt the most inappropriate version of what you deem acceptable.

The reality is, I'm not the Claudia Schiffer version of hot mums across social media, and more often than not people laugh at me, not with me. As my son, you are probably going to have an issue with that at some point in your life and I get that. I hope you will grow up to understand that the reasons your stupid mum did dickhead things on the internet was because she wanted women to feel empowered, brave and no longer ashamed of how they look, or how they feel.

I haven't always kept my patience and I've lost my temper way too many times. I have got things wrong and I've said I'm sorry. I'm not perfect, but there is one thing I've always been so sure of and that is I always wanted to be a mum, even when I was a little girl. This job has been so much more challenging than I had ever anticipated and I've questioned whether I am doing an awful job on so many occasions, but all it'll ever come down to is how grateful I am that you are my son.

You have given me so much happiness and you've given me the confidence to be this person, because you've always just loved me. Even on my bad days when I've felt like the least lovable person, I've still been your knight in shining armour. I want you to know you don't have to fear the unknown, you just have to believe that no matter where that road takes you, I will be there. There have been times in your life where I've been sick, and maybe as that adult you'll remember the snippets where we had to move in with Nanna and Granddad and how I didn't act like your mum for a while. Once I got better and got back in the saddle, I made a promise to myself, and to you, which was to always be your biggest cheerleader. I have guided you, I have been that mum who fiercely protects you and I will go on to be the person who claps the loudest with the biggest tears of joy in my eyes, because loving you now is

not only so easy, but such a wonderful feeling, one
that will never be lost on me again.

I have spent so many years wandering around
life feeling utterly petrified by the fear of what
others thought. But eventually I realised my life isn't
here to be wasted on other people's thoughts, and
more importantly I wanted you and your brother
to understand the importance of walking to the
beat of your own drum. My hope is you continue to
laugh so much it makes me feel sick, that you carry
on making friends as easily as you do, that you
never stop having that much to say (you literally
never stop talking), and that you love life, because
watching you grow up has so far been a true
privilege and honour.

I'll love you always,

Mum x

Taking the perfect family photo is like trying to arrange angry bears in an orderly line; one of them is picking their nose and the other is touching their penis, while Steve blinks at the exact moment the flash goes.

8

Goodnight, Jimbob – goodnight, you little arsehole

School runs and skid marks

Picture it: you're in the middle of the supermarket, your kid is trying to summon the devil, you're wondering if it's acceptable to walk away and hope another family finds him, when a lady approaches you to say, 'It gets easier, you know.' Like, seriously Brenda, I've been told 40 million fucking times it gets easier, but how about you go and buy me a bottle of wine, give me a cheeky slap on the arse and tell me it's okay that my kid is a prick, because everyone has been there. You are the mum who left the baby days, kissed the toddler years goodbye and you're still faced with the same shit. How is this fair? Brenda, before you do fuck off can you actually give me a rough time frame of when I should expect this to end? Just coz I'm a little confused how I can have a seven-year-old still pulling identical crap.

Every single parent has seen their kid throw it down a fuckload of times in public, and yet, when it's your kid, everyone acts like you're a shit mum who can't keep her kid under control. No mate, this thing I birthed, he is feral. Don't get me wrong, I am smug as fuck when it's my kid who's behaving and isn't the one throwing a random Clark's shoe in the frozen peas section as this poor bitch continually picks it up because those shoes aren't cheap. I am human and I celebrate the small moments when my kids act like something out of *The Waltons*, but I'm not so far up my own arse as to be unable to recognise when sometimes those adults related to said fuckbags just need a reassuring arm squeeze to say 'You got this, babe!', without adding the words 'IT DOES GET BETTER'. Or, for that matter, 'Wait until they're teenagers.'

I feel sad, confused and honestly just mindfucked by the parent who chooses to portray family life as perfect. Why? Mainly because I am yet to meet a perfect human being, let alone a perfect family. And yet, for some, I've noticed it is so important for their family to be seen as untouchable, like their daughter never acts like a total knob. It makes me start to question my own family set-up. Thoughts include: 'What the Jesus, hell and Christ have I done wrong, because as their child sits nicely colouring in, mine is rubbing his penis along the window and making fart noises?!'

Our desire to hide the penis-rubbing, fart-making, deranged child and the equally deranged parenting behind it is overwhelming.

I have spent so many years wondering if their little outbursts of having a massive shit fit in public represent my ability to parent them. For some reason, when my kids are doing the knee skids throughout the supermarket (with me begging them to stop), all the other kids appear to be behaving. Why is that? How is it when my kids are being total douchebags, I am completely unable to see past the fact that all kids have their moments? I always envisaged trips to the supermarket together to be special, letting them choose a cake for good behaviour as Steve and I stroll hand in hand. We don't though, and

more often than not we are dragging them out of clothing rails as they slap the other with the first pair of pants
they find down the underwear aisle.

I find a trip to the supermarket on my own a lot like
a minibreak; it feels orgasmic to look at the cheese aisle
without yelling at the kids to not get in the way of other
people or to stop fighting. I know this whole phase will
end and eventually the simple job of going food shopping together in peace will happen, and I'll wish for
these stressful days back, but genuinely there are days
when I feel so completely done in by being their parent
that I just wish for a time where I don't constantly question how the fuck I am still getting back up for more!?!

You know, I want future me to pop by and let Steve
and me know that the kids grew up to be good people –
they never went on to be axe murderers, and they are
capable of loving without being narcissistic pricks – but
mainly I just want future me to let me know we made it
out the other side alive. That for all the tantrums where
I lost a small piece of my soul, or the moments where I
shouted so much my neighbours stood to attention, we
didn't truly completely fuck it all up.

I remember, after having Toby, telling Steve it wouldn't
be long before we didn't feel so tired. That very soon
from now this whole job would become a lot easier, and
we would find that balance. I'm not sure if I read that in
some bullshit magazine or if I made it up, but it turns

out that is utter crap. We are now five years into being parents of two children and it is still just as demanding.

How the fuck is that possible? Surely they can do more now, and that should make this job easier? They can put their own shoes on, they tell you they love you, they can openly communicate their feelings and they cry less ... Yet I am still having to wipe their arses! How? Why? Surely that wasn't part of this contract? You know, like how the fuck am I still having to inspect another person's arsehole more than my own?

I expected the baby days to be hard, and the early stages – like when they learn to walk and open shit they shouldn't touch – to be tough but why does it carry on? The challenges of trying to remind a child that it's important to wash their penis every single day and not just on the occasion when you feel like it? I always thought I would have the children who didn't fight, I just knew they would get along.

The boys have a wonderful relationship, but I'd be lying if I said that, in the almost five short years they've been brothers, blood hasn't been spilled. Elliott is a huge Minecraft fan, and with that comes all the shit merchandise that literally does fuck all other than take space up in your house. Elliott decided to play with his Minecraft axe, and – to be sure he gave the full effect of wielding such an incredible toy – he flung it over his back with all his might, like his life depended on it. Only problem was, his brother was stood behind him.

Toby's top lip sprayed blood as Elliott stood there and said, 'Whoops ...' He sounded sincere but anyone who has ever hurt their sibling knows that 'whoops' refers to the whole world of shit they are about to be in. Never in my life have I seen Elliott be so attentive, getting my kitchen roll and trying to make his brother laugh. He sounds cute, but the reality was he knew he was in so much fucking trouble once his brother stopped spitting blood over the living room carpet. I think this is what you call damage limitation.

There's no denying having two is fucking hard work, and yet they love each other. They can beat the shit out of each other, but no one else can. As they grow older how much they love each other only becomes more evident. When Elliott cries because someone has upset him, Toby cries. He loves his big brother so much. Unfortunately, when Toby cries, Elliott just laughs – that whole empathy thing skipped him completely.

I sometimes cry at the sheer frustration of how they can elbow each other every single time we get to the car 'in the hope that they can be the one to get to the door first and open it.' I honestly want to shout 'STOP BEING FUCKING WANKERS!' because it is without a doubt one of the many things about having more than one child that is annoying as shit, but they never seem to care about Mummy having a nervous breakdown because it happens more often than I care to mention. They can't share with each other and that's not because they are incapable of the basic human instinct; they manage it just fine with their mates. I'm pretty sure they just do it to piss me off, as they come to moan at me that the other one isn't giving a blue Lego brick back at 6am – mate, I don't give a flying pig's dick! Find another toy and leave me the fuck alone until at least 7.30.

Toby looks up to Elliott like he's the absolute dog's whangers. He tries to copy him, he likes to hang around with his friends (much to Elliott's disgust), and, every single weekend, he climbs out of his bed and straight into Elliott's room to sit next to him. Elliott is the big brother when it counts, always protecting him instinctively if another kid is horrible, or if he needs his yogurt opening, sharing the blanket when they watch the TV, which always reduces me to tears because those little moments alone are enough to keep me going through the times where I want to (and often do) actually lose my shit at them, because I know it's the making of a lifelong friendship.

When I was younger, I only had to breathe near my sister and she'd threaten me with death, and yet when she was once worried I was being bullied at school, she talked me through how to punch hard and fast. Pretty sure my parents weren't aware of that sisterly bonding session we shared. But we fought a lot. In fact, so much so that I remember being stood at the bottom of the stairs, screaming at her to go get fucked, as she stood at the top of the stairs and bellowed for me to come up there and say it to her face (absolutely no fucking way I had any intentions of doing that because I'm all mouth). My mum, who was sat in the living room, got up, and I thought in that moment, 'YES!! Emma is about to get in a world of shit for threatening me!' But, instead, Mum shut the door. She SHUT THE DOOR. Never in my life has my anal sphincter spasmed so fast as when I saw my sister start to come down the stairs, so I belted it out the front door and vowed to find a new family because my sister would no doubt have me in a headlock as soon as I walked back through the threshold. I couldn't believe it, my mum ... SHUT the fucking DOOR. Like she didn't care! Truth was, she didn't because she had totally had a gutful and I really get that now. Sometimes, for your own sanity, you just have to assume until there is blood, shit or vomit, they just need to fight it out themselves.

Roll forwards to now and, all those fights we had, they're laughable. There were so many I honestly can't count them. But Emma is my best friend; she protects me and loves me like her own daughter at times, even though I'm a full-grown adult. I look up to her, and I honestly adore her because even throughout the times I told her I absolutely hated her, I never ever did. That's why I know Elliott and Toby will one day be okay, because if my relationship with my sister is anything to go by they will go on to be incredibly blessed to have each other.

'They have voluntary deafness. Don't touch it – they fucking touch it! Move away from it – so they go fucking closer. Don't eat that – you know they bloody will!'

The challenge of being a parent to older children is remembering they will remember the moments you fucked up and will be sure to remind you once they're older. It's knowing that sometimes they are miniature versions of yourself and the one thing you hate about their mouth and attitude is how much it sounds and looks like what you used to do. Ain't that a bitch, and not to mention they absolutely know when you've skipped a page in that book you read at night-time. Doesn't sound like a big deal but when your Chinese takeaway is downstairs going cold, you kind of want that last page to hurry the fuck up. And now you have a kid who listens and understands EVERYTHING you say.

During my whimsically pregnant and ignorant days, I hadn't forward-thought about how much they need you and for how long. I didn't see the long game – does anyone?? The endless washing (how is there that many clothes??), the backchat, the years of early starts, the complete and utter lack of picking up after themselves (like every kid does it and it doesn't matter how many times you say, don't fucking do that, they keep on doing it). They have voluntary deafness. Don't touch it – they fucking touch it! Move away from it – so they go fucking closer. Don't eat that – you know they bloody will!

My mum would always get pissed off at me for not tidying my room, while I mused that I'd always be that awesome mum with no rules and kick-ass bedtime stories. Roll forwards to now, as I angrily hoover their bedroom floors wondering how the fuck they manage to make that much mess and make a carpet look like one massive wank rag. I am now my mother, and that is sobering while also tragic, because I now realise what a total jumped-up prick I was for assuming she knew shit all about absolutely everything as even the sound of her breathing made me want to rip my skin off.

I remember my mum was trying to save our local hospital (being an absolute legend, but at the time it felt like she was being a total prick). It was an old military one that won awards for its level of excellence, but who needs a fucking hospital, right?? Fuck no, so of course the government closed it and during its appeal period my mum was at the forefront of making sure everyone knew how disgusted she was about this. She printed posters with bold capitals saying 'SAVE HASLAR HOSPITAL' and stuck them in every window-pane of the house for everyone to see. I'm unsure if she thought carrier pigeons would deliver this message to 10 Downing Street, but I do know my dad was pissed off she used a whole ink cartridge on these fucking

things. And I died a million deaths. What was this
woman doing to me?? IN EVERY SINGLE FUCKING
WINDOW??

I was the 14-year-old girl who wore compressed
orange powder foundation that you could get for a quid
from the local Saturday market, and I was the one with
the issue?!? I mean, I think someone should have had a
word, to be honest, but I didn't talk to her for a week. I
was appalled she was drawing so much attention to our
house, to my life. How fucking embarrassing!

I am now that mum who sees her son roll his eyes
when I sing to my incredibly awesome rock 'n' roll
music and cover his face when I dance. I'm fast becoming the poster-printing mum wanker who will go on to
ruin their teenage years with the things I am passion-
ate about, and all the while I stand and watch them
make the same hideous fashion decisions I once did
while silently judging, just like my mum did over the
tangoed knob of a daughter she was in possession of
back then.

We are all the poster wanker at some point, because,
as we get older, we find our feet a little more and we find
the confidence to fight back; it's amazing and liberat-
ing, but all the while totally hideously embarrassing for
any children associated with you. It is a rite of passage
for a child to, at some point or another, fucking hate
their parents, while being blissfully unaware of their
own shit-awful decisions being pretty mortifying to live

with as a parent. Sometimes parents will embarrass you by their very existence. That whole 'you should be grateful they brought you into this world' doesn't cut it because you're just too busy looking at your mates' parents, wishing yours were that cool. Not once realising that, mate, he feels the same about your mum and dad.

All it comes down to is, no matter if it's the toddler or the teen, we are all in the same boat. Waiting for the appropriate moment for their back to be turned so we can stick our middle finger up at them! We pray for their bedtime to allow ourselves that fleeting moment where we can sit in our pyjamas, braless, eating the chocolate we have hidden from them all day and remembering a time when we had less grey hair and perkier tits. If I didn't have these simple self-help techniques, and that of a well-timed 'fuck you' under my breath, I don't even know how I would be surviving right now.

> *'We keep hold of our children for longer.*
> *We don't send them out into the big scary*
> *world like they did when I was a kid.*
> *It means we are with them every single*
> *waking hour of every single day and that*
> *is hard work!'*

It's funny how the older generation are so quick to say 'in our day this' and 'in our day that'. Yes, love, in your

day we were booted out of the door in the morning,
allowed home at lunch and then back out until dinner
as you polished your brass fucking fireplace and
hoovered 14 times a day! You are right, maybe our
children don't visit the park as often, but I absolutely
never saw you over there keeping a watchful eye on
your little shitbags as they terrorised the local fields
as we do.

Things have changed. We keep hold of our children
for longer. We don't send them out into the big scary
world like they did when I was a kid. It means we are
with them every single waking hour of every single
day and that is hard work! I wouldn't change it – quite
honestly, when my children are allowed out of the house
without me I will no doubt ask Steve to slip me a seda-
tive because I won't cope with it at all. The point is,
we don't check out of parenting, and that is truly why
I believe tablets and games consoles were invented. I
am so thankful for that little bastard 'screen time' – it
is the most powerful thing we own. One single threat of
losing their screen time and all of a sudden my children
go from teabagging demons to delicate angels who open
doors for each other.

I once heard a non-parent announce on the radio
that parents should simply stop their children from
using technology and give them a book. Mate, until you
smell like I do, have the bags under your eyes like I have
and walk in the shoes of a parent who is tired, hungry

and just desperate for a break, please do not offer us the solution of a book. Do you really think we didn't try that?? You can buy a book for 50p in the local charity shop, and that's a dickload cheaper than the crap we end up having to buy.

I have found a well-placed thumb up one's arse can prevent the accidental slip of assuming we know what works for everyone. I don't even know what I'm having for dinner each night; so how the fuck am I meant to know what someone else is doing with their children?? It is the whole 'told you so' ethos: they wait with bated breath for the first sign that whatever decision you made is a monumental fuck-up and they relish the idea that they knew all along it was wrong. Steve and I have been on the receiving end of this on so many occasions. We have nodded, smiled and then gone home utterly horrified we made the worst decision and will go on to create adults who will blame us because we put them to bed at 7pm when in fact the parenting gods had said you should do it at 7.30.

To start with, most of our parental decisions were down to Google. Yes, there were the odd occasions when I've googled an illness to which the answer has come back that basically our child has four hours left to live, but mostly we looked at the pros and cons of whatever we weren't sure on. Eventually, we just started using our gut to make the decision: 'Could this kill him?? No! Then fuck it, let's do it!'

> *'Sometimes we're so heavily entwined in their lives we feel invisible to them, but … know that the ship would sink without us, the smiles would quickly disappear into tears and there would literally be shit on the walls.'*

I remember a while ago putting Elliott to bed and, as he begged as always for Steve, I asked, like an absolute idiot, 'Do you prefer Daddy being around over Mummy?' I assured him it was okay because I wouldn't lose my temper if he told me the truth. He replied, 'Yeah,' and I silently paused for a while and thought about it. 'If you had a choice, would you prefer Mummy went to work all the time? And Daddy stayed home with you?' And it was a massive kick to the chuff when he replied, 'Yes, I wish you went to work.'

Fuck!

That hurt. I kissed him goodnight and I went downstairs. I then proceeded to cry because I hadn't spent 36 hours of labour to push his fat head out of my vagina only to be told years later Steve basically could have done it better. I gave it all up for them, career, body, gallbladder (losing an organ five years after birth can still be considered his fault), my memory, my ability to shave bodily hair on a regular basis, and I've done it gladly (especially the body hair bit), but to our boys Steve is on a pedestal. He is the untouchable cool dad who makes them laugh, finds new fun games and ignites their imagination.

I stand in the wings waiting to be called in, but I never am. So I just hang around like the third wheel on a date, fingering my arsehole, laughing even though I don't get any of the jokes. Sometimes that shit flies because, I guess, I'm never not there for them. Then there are other times when it feels like the only thing that's flying is pebble-dashed diarrhoea in the face.

I've kicked ass at school, I've defended them when kids push them around, I constantly nurture their personality so they won't feel the pathetic expectations of society to 'act like a man', and let them be who they want to be. I wipe their arses and dry their eyes when it all goes a bit tits up. I'm good at always being there, but that makes me pretty boring. I've always known they love Daddy to put them to bed because he's their hero. I'm more the silent partner who does the end-of-month accounts.

So I cried; I cried so much that I turned on Steve, blaming him for all the ways he is better than me. I love him! And I also hate him! I hate him because I want to be him! I know they couldn't live without me; I'm their mum and I kiss away pains like no one else in their lives. Sometimes, kids, it wouldn't hurt to fight over me, rather than kick me in the tits as you scramble off the sofa to get to him first. They act like I'm a venereal disease they're trying not to catch.

I want to be begged to do bedtime (while also very aware having spent a whole fucking day with them I wouldn't want to put them to bed anyway). I want to be begged to stay home and I want those smiles when I walk through the door. Instead, I have to constantly tell myself how important I am to them – how, when the shit hits the fan, they come running to me because they know as well as I do that I'm like a lioness with her cubs and this bitch doesn't fuck about.

We all have a role to play in the lives of those we love the most. We might not always seem relevant, feel appreciated and we might not always understand it, but it'll always be hugely important. Sometimes we're so heavily entwined in their lives we feel invisible to them, but it's important to remember being part of the furniture doesn't make us boring, invisible and unwanted. It makes us reliable, loved, wanted and needed. We are the heroes, and while it might be the unspoken and undervalued job, know that the ship would sink without us, the smiles would quickly disappear into tears and there would literally be shit on the walls.

Don't get me wrong, I love to relinquish my responsibility of being their parent from time to time. I will pretend to be in the middle of something important, I'll act like I'm cleaning, or sometimes I'll pretend to be in a really bad mood just so Steve understands without the words being spoken that he is absolutely putting the kids to bed. I find bedtime the worst – they're tired, so are you, they don't listen, you have to scream, while wondering how you became that mum!?! You just don't want to read *The Gruffalo* for the ninetieth time because you know he has purple prickles all over his back and honestly you don't give a shit and wish your kid would pick another story. They never do, and I'm undecided if it's because they like the predictability of the same thing night in, night out, or if it's the personal enjoyment of watching a little piece of your soul being crushed as you make your way through what the snake, fox and fucking owl said to the little brown mouse.

Like most things we tag team the worst bits, but sometimes I will just ignore them as they wrestle! On the ground! In the park! As people watch! And judge!

Truth be told, I get to a point where I am no longer giving a shit when I have already told them 90 times to stop doing it, and they're ignoring every fucking word I've said and are doing it anyway. As I watch Steve trying to regain control, looking at me with those wild eyes – like 'Will you actually come and help?!?' – I never do; I sit watching, while inwardly wondering what it must be like to have sex with Keanu Reeves and going to my happy place. I believe that if we didn't have those places someone would die, because you check out of life to survive. We aren't being bad mums.

– To the awesome single – – parents,

Single parents, I just don't even understand
how you do it. The moment where no one else
is coming through the door. The fact there is no
person falling into a heap on the sofa with you
to talk about your day. The level of loneliness
must be all-consuming at times and yet no one is
giving you much recognition for it. If they wake
in the night, there is no other person to kick out
of bed and force to take care of the child and I
wish I could put into words the level of respect I
have for that.

We all think we could manage it until we're
faced with those shit days – you know, where
something has crawled up their arse, or your
arse, or even both, and you're just done, but you
don't have the choice to be done because they
need to be bathed, they need to be fed and they
need to be tucked up in bed. How do you do
those days? I get it, you survive them just like
everyone else, but I just want to take a moment
to say: 'Well done!' You are overdue a hug; I just
know it. You haven't had a proper cooked meal in
too long and you are the definition of a walking
mombie (*to all the single men, walking dadbi?*

... yeah, that doesn't work), you aren't even sure how you put one foot in front of each other but you do. My admiration goes out to all men and women who do this job with no one at their side to step in when they've had enough.

That is the truth of it: we all, at some point, sometimes regularly, have enough of being the responsible adult and we just want to sit on the sofa, refusing to commit to this life. You are amazing at simply keeping these kids alive all on your own.

The Mother's and Father's Days where no one gives you the card to say 'I love you'. And yet on those days when no dad or mum is there, for whatever reason, you still make that day special for your kids because you don't want them to feel any lack of love from that other parent not being around.

If you haven't resorted to a heavy dependency on alcohol you are absolutely doing a better job of this than I would be. (*I am also not encouraging the use of alcohol to get through your days as a parent. While I am no expert, I believe the long-term effects of alcoholism aren't ideal.*) In short, you rock, but you are way too busy to notice that because you have a million plates to keep spinning. I am sorry for every single moment you miss out, cry alone, feel like you are sinking and never ever being given the recognition you deserve. I am sorry for all the hugs you haven't been given when the days are too long to cope with but please remember this – it's all worth it. They aren't saying it right now, but for all the times you put them first, that you show them the love of two parents and you never ever stop trying, just know they will thank you. That in itself is enough to hold on out and wait for. Also remember, you are fucking wonderful.

'How can we expect them to make it out alive if even their farts are measured by levels of success?'

I *love* the school run – having to be up and out of the house before I've even had a chance to wash my vagina or eat anything, while socialising with other mums, hoping no one can smell my rancid breath – about as much as I enjoy an anal exam. You think you'll be thankful for when your child finally starts school, but when the day arrives where you have to wave them off into the scary world of school, where you hope they've wiped their arse properly and their teacher isn't a total witch who makes them cry, you feel a very large hole carved into your heart that aches as they disappear into the classroom. I always thought I'd be that Mum, because truly those four years of farm visits and cuddles on the sofa had whizzed by my eyes and I was suddenly the owner of a schoolchild. How did that happen? But sadly for Elliott, Mummy didn't give a fuck and I completely skipped the part where I felt heartbroken. He had gone to school and I had a four-week-old baby, a heavy dependency on sleeping tablets, undiagnosed postnatal depression, along with a gallbladder that was pickling itself and a liver that was slowly failing.

But I quickly went back to mum of two: doing the school run, dry shampoo barely brushed through my hair and a baby I never got dressed out of his pyjamas. It became a joke for some of the playground parents as Toby reached 18 months and was still in his bedtime onesie in the morning. I smiled while inwardly telling them to all get fucked. Dressing myself and one child was enough. He was clothed, wasn't he? Somehow I managed to make it on time, while having one kid hanging off me like a limpet and begging me not to send him in. This whole being a mum in the playground gig sucked arse; all you ever did was pick up irrational, tired children who constantly told you the teacher was better, or cooler or kinder.

Your kids don't know their arse from their elbow at this point in their lives, yet suddenly they are being taxed in every single capacity: sitting at tables, being silent, playing and then all of a sudden learning their ABCs, as we are told as parents what a correct phonetic sound is. You don't half feel like a giant penis when sat in a hall with 90 other parents learning the letter SSSSS. We get it. Thanks!

These tiny people literally haven't a fucking clue and yet we drop-kick them into full-time education barely able to hold a pencil and they're told, 'Now write and please know we will silently be judging your ability and reporting back to Mummy and Daddy about how your handwriting looks like a slug's penis just smeared across the page.' It enrages me because we expect so much of them and while I was absolutely desperate to lose one of the kids for a few hours a day, the reality was he just wasn't ready! At all! He took years before we actually managed to settle into the rhythm of school. And some kids never do – they aren't able to cope with the structure, the routine. While we celebrate individuality in adults, we expect children to walk the thin blue line of what is deemed acceptable.

Emotional needs aren't always met – it is impossible, mainly because the classes are big, and the staff are stretched to maximum capacity. The teachers have pages and PAGES of things to mark, and a long line of children to assess to make sure they are meeting county guidelines. So we raise an army of kids who are bound by the school rules, government testing and homework that even I have to look up. Elliott once got homework about fractions – I got an F for my maths GCSE, I was probably never going to be the right person to ask because I'm pretty sure to be graded an F you haven't even spelt your name right! I guessed the answers, but I did it confidently. He hugged me and said, 'Thank you, Mummy, you're the best.' That week he got every single question wrong on his homework, but I realised that while I believe it's always good to apply yourself in school and work hard for what you want, somehow this F-grading, dyslexic bellend hasn't done too badly.

In actual fact, instead of scaremongering children around SATs, GCSEs (or whatever the fuck they call them now), spelling tests and fucking fractions, we should be telling them that the most important thing they can do is try their best and forget the rest. No child can be amazing at every single subject and yet there we are in parents' evening being told they have to work harder because they aren't where they should be! I don't blame the teachers, I have met many who completely disagree with the pressure put on children, and so for that reason I'm absolutely fine with knowing that some weeks we won't get around to doing that spelling test, or doing that maths homework, because I am going to take them to the park instead – where they will run around like lunatics and

I will shout and lose my shit that they won't listen, but mainly I'll let them be free of all the pressures we put on children nowadays. How can we expect them to make it out alive if even their farts are measured by levels of success?

I will continue to rebel against the system when they tell me I can't take my child out of school on holiday because I'm ruining their education, because I believe a classroom is incapable of providing a full complement of adventure, family time and life experiences.

I see children practising their music and their parents pushing them to excel while boasting that they are moving up reading bands and how they're proud, and I'm pleased for them. Truly, I am. But I also just don't give a shit, because that kid you are pushing and pushing at some point or another will combust; whether that means becoming a teenager who repeatedly drinks themselves into an alcoholic stupor, or gets a face tattoo of a wolf howling at the moon, all that pressure at some point is going to pour out of them like steam from a train. We want what is best for them, but mainly I just want them to be happy, and if that is picking their nose and eating it, who am I to judge? I just ask they do it when I'm not looking because, while I'm a laid-back mum with regards to their extracurricular activities, watching someone chow down on their nose dwellers is where I draw a line.

> *'These kids are so much more hardcore
> than adults. We can really fuck them
> around and yet they never stay down
> when they're knocked. They continue to
> get up. How do we lose that fight as we fall
> into adulthood?'*

Being a mum with a child in school means you have to be ready for drama, because kids are going to fall out with each other daily. One minute you're going to want to kick the shit out of one kid only to find the next day they are now alright and it's another child who now sounds like a bit of a dickhead. Take it from me, it's probably best to just nod and agree with your child's outpouring, while making a mental note of the problem kid's name for future reference, but do not stare them down in the playground – their parents never take kindly to it ... ever.

Elliott is very sensitive; I love that about him but it also means he can hold a grudge longer than the Gallagher brothers. I found myself totally embroiled in whatever the fuck it is that happens in break time, and waiting with dread at the school gates at the end of the day for a roundup of who was out of favour on that particular day. I found this hard, really hard in fact, because unlike those days where you could choose who they hung around with and make sure they avoided Shovey Shane, your child is now let loose into the lion's den of the schoolyard, where other children might not have the same morals and might like to pick on their peers for how they look or what they wear.

There have been so many times in his short five years in school where I have spent the night awake agonising over how sad he is because of other children treating him badly. I know he isn't a saint – he always makes out his shit doesn't stink, but, if his attitude in the mornings is anything to go by, I imagine he also does things that hurt other children. Of course he does; he's a kid and the whole way we learn in life is through fucking up, invariably being bollocked for it and then remembering to not do it again because it turns out that was a bad idea.

When Elliott was moving from Infants to Juniors we made the decision to move schools. He suffered with anxiety, and his first school wasn't ever able to cope with his needs. I was often left in the playground with him crying and begging me not to leave him, and no one ever came to help, or if they did he was just ripped off of me and told to stop being silly. It was such a tough decision to change schools because we knew he wouldn't know anyone, and yet he coped way better than I could have expected.

It was incredibly humbling and heartbreaking to watch, because I saw this tiny human doing something many adults couldn't manage. He knew no one and yet he tried his best to introduce himself to people: 'Hello, my name is Elliott. What is your name?'

His first taster session at the new school ended with him being laughed at for the way he ran. It bothered him so much that the whole of the summer holidays he didn't run if anyone else was around, yet he never stopped trying to run faster when we were alone with him, and I choked on tears to see his determination to keep on trying.

His first day in the new school I barely held it together. I was a mess. I cried with pride, fear and anxiety because I knew what an incredible kid he was. That broken mess who didn't give a shit in Reception was gone and replaced with this person who couldn't even describe the emotions flowing through his body. I was in turmoil, and it actually felt good to have that feeling. It reminded me that: babe, you might not have your shit together but these tears show you have come a long way. I just needed these new children to see in Elliott what a lovely little boy he was. I needed him to make friends because I knew what it felt like to be the new person somewhere desperate to just fit in.

It took him such a long time to settle. Each morning he would have to go into school via the reception desk because he couldn't cope with the noise, hustle and bustle of the playground. He would often cry when I had to leave and beg me to stay. At no point in our job as mother is it easy to walk away from your baby as they sob for you not to go. No matter how old they are, your instinct is to stay.

I always thought that as kids got older it got easier, like you almost loved them slightly less because they go through the ugly stage – you know, the one where they lose teeth and smile like they just snorted cocaine, all wide-eyed and frantic. Turns out you don't stop loving them during the ugly stage. And just for your information, you don't look at your own gappy-toothed children and think they look ugly; you just think that about everyone else's child. Do not tell me you haven't thought it because we all know it's true!

Thankfully moving Elliott was the best decision we ever made; he has been nurtured and cared for in the way we had always hoped. He has come on in leaps and bounds, no longer that kid who can't cope with the play-ground while also being the little boy who never looks back because, in his words, 'Mummy, if I look back I know I will cry and I won't want to leave you.' His level of bravery is something I will never get tired of seeing. For a boy who struggles with anxiety, this is tough; he doesn't like the unexpected, he needs so much reassurance and he has been known to root himself to the spot and cry if he can't cope with his surroundings. We have had to carry him as he has sobbed into our shoulders and as his parents that's okay. Being there for him in those moments feels more of a privilege than a chore because I can see how far he has come. It'll never feel humiliating because his relationship with us means he's strong enough to show his weakness, knowing we will do everything we can to protect him.

These kids are so much more hardcore than adults. We can really fuck them around and yet they never stay down when they're knocked. They continue to get up. How do we lose that fight as we fall into adulthood? As kids we all went through such turmoil, such massive change, and in those early years we hit each wave with such determination and fight. As a mother it is amazing to see a child who is scared of the dark and doesn't like places with loud noises just keep on giving it a good go.

I have learnt through Elliott that for every stumbling block we face in life, it's not about trying to find a way around it, but running at it with all your might and believing you won't jump over it, but knock that bastard flying. We all face challenges, even kids do, but sometimes we could learn a thing or two from the simplicity of how they deal with it.

-Laura's Life Lesson - - - - -

When they're older, they will, for the most part, be thankful for all the shit you do right now that they completely take for granted. Because no child will ever be aware of how many times you've had to drive to the Co-op in your slippers to buy toilet roll because they are mid-shit and you have nothing to wipe their arse with. When they are older and have gone through the wanky

teenage years where they just despise you, as
you equally detest the very presence of their
oversized attitude, what you will be left with are
these really awesome people who become a bit
like friends. You enjoy their company and they
just say thank you for always being there. I mean,
if that isn't how this whole parental thing pans
out then I want my money back!! What a fucker
these kids don't come with a gift receipt.

Parenting truths

* You are always expected to be the snack bitch. Ain't nothing getting away from the fact. When they say they're hungry you best be packing something, otherwise be prepared for level expert of the pisser and moaner.

* 'Uugghhhh, when does it end?' I hear you cry. The worry, anguish, tiredness and responsibility? Well, I'm here to tell you the good news … when you die.

* Nope, you aren't getting it right because none of us are. Now stop crying, find some chocolate, hide from the kids and give yourself a minute to remember even the queen has told Charles to fuck off at some point.

* Sometimes you aren't going to agree with your husband's decision and you are going to overrule him. If that hasn't happened yet, take it from my personal experience, it goes down as well as a wet fart in a public swimming pool.

* Try not to be the wanky mum who pushes other kids out the way because you think yours is better than everyone else's. No one is saying it, but, trust me, they all think you're a twat. Pipe down and get to the back of the fucking queue.

�֍ Even when they're teenagers you can't leave the
bastards alone out of fear they'll throw a party
while you're gone.

�֍ 'Sweet baby Jesus, you were born with perfectly
good eyes and will you just fucking look for it
yourself and stop telling me you can't fucking find it.'
Often heard echoing around the walls of my house.

�֍ If you don't threaten them with every single
thing that might make them behave – Father
Christmas isn't coming, you won't be going on
holiday or, my old favourite, you won't get any
pudding if you don't eat your dinner – are you
even a mum?!?!

�֍ My hobbies include never being able to pair
socks, smelling someone else's pants to see
if they smell like piss and very rarely getting
the opportunity to have sex with my husband
because I'm too exhausted.

✤ Siblings fight, let them. Close the door and know
they do love each other enough that if one of
them is unconscious they will be sure to come
and tell you.

✤ Do not feel bad for wanting a break and wishing
they could just fuck off for a night. If that thought
process isn't normal, then someone is going to
need to break that one to me gently as I've spent
the last nine years always living for the nights
when my parents babysit.

✳ They truly don't understand the phrase, 'Just
leave me alone!' No matter their age, I have come
to realise I may never take a shit in peace again.

✳ Even when it feels like the days are impossibly
long, just give yourself a pat on the back. You're
still there, well done. That in itself is amazing.

Darling Husband

Dear Steve,

Look, it only took 18 years of putting up with my shit and listening to my endless complaints of how you don't wash the bottom of glasses out properly to feature in a book. You lucky prick, not a lot of husbands can say that, which means I will remind you of this moment in all future arguments.

I just want to say thank you – not just for taking the photos where you see the exact place my gooch was stitched back up post-birth, but thank you for being the constant support in my life. You never tell me anything is too much, you never dampen my dreams and you always remind me to believe in myself. That 17-year-old girl who kept asking if someone had paid you to date me (I had clearly watched *10 Things I Hate About You* too much to believe that shit actually happens in real life, only you're not as hot as Heath Ledger was in that movie ... awkward), who didn't believe in herself at all, felt so ugly and worthless that she could never understand why someone like you would be interested in someone like her. Well, I guess I must suck like a hoover because you're still here, and, considering I've not given you a blow job in about

three years, it must ultimately come down to the fact
I do make a cracking Victoria sponge cake.

We aren't always getting it right as husband and
wife, and I know there are days where we just exist
in each other's presence because the boys take up so
much of our time. Sometimes I just miss that hug, or
the kiss that doesn't lead to you spooning my back
with an erection. I just sometimes miss the contact,
because in amongst the chaos of being married we
are raising two incredibly demanding children who
never relent. I'm sorry that in some respects we
have lost each other, but one day, not far from now,
the hand-holding, the kissing (that doesn't lead to
erections) and hugs will return, but the difference
will be those little people who once hung on our
every word will be gone and the fury of where they
once ran at each other like two fighting elephants
will be over and replaced with an echoed silence.
Something I know I will miss, even if it drives me
fucking mental now.

While we can always promise to kiss more
tomorrow, let's cling on to these final moments of
our children being young enough that they enjoy our
company. Before we know it, all we'll have is each
other, and, while I can't wait for those days, I'm
also aware you will no doubt annoy the shit out of
me and I'll be in a state of permanent depression,
wishing to have children hanging off my arms asking

for more snacks. To sum up, you are fucked either
way!!

Thank you for being my everything and for loving
me beyond measure. Thanks for being my equal
and not seeing me as the lesser human because
I own a vagina. And thank you for continuing to
begrudgingly take the stupid photos, appear in my
videos and for being my biggest cheerleader. While I
do believe you are a dickhead who can sometimes get
it wrong by just breathing, you are *my* dickhead and
I wouldn't change you ... unless I could turn you into
Keanu Reeves.

Laura

Darling Wife

Laura,

So, this is weird and I guess for once in my life I have the floor to just speak openly without you interrupting me. Do I need to mention all the times you forget to put your sanitary towels in the bin and leave them wrapped up on the side like little presents that no one wants to open?? Or is that too much? Maybe I should mention that time you once shouted at me because I 'WASN'T EVEN TRYING TO GET THE CAMERA ANGLE RIGHT!!' ... Probably best I leave that one out too, huh?!?!

Being your husband is great, challenging, exhausting, and I'm not even including the kids in all of that. Watching you grow from the person who lay in bed each night sobbing that you wanted to die to see you now – all naked, bad mouthed but smiling – feels a bit of an honour, because there have been moments of my life where I've been so sure I'd lose you for ever. In short it's good to have you back, and I appreciate you carry those scars around with you, but it's been a pleasure to watch you grow into this person. I can't say I've always loved the idea of thousands of people seeing half of my wife's tit displayed across social media to be laughed at, especially the thought of another man keeping it for his own personal wank bank, but I guess the awesome thing you've done is make people smile as well as giving me an opportunity to see you naked more often. I just sometimes wish it didn't include your vagina being smeared up against a pane of glass in our conservatory for all our neighbours to see.

I'm not sure what's next? If the last 18 years are anything to go by, I imagine it'll be pretty chaotic. This isn't the life I thought we would have, and if someone had told me ten years ago that you'd be where you are now, having gone through everything you have, I'd have laughed and told them to fuck off. Yet, here I am most evenings watching you grind the bannister rail so much so I wonder if that thing will ever recover from being that far up your vag.

We don't know what's next, but I hope it only continues to make you smile, because that is by far the very best thing you wear, other than those lace knickers you bust out for special occasions.

Thank you for being completely unpredictable and totally mental. I wouldn't change a single bit of it.

Love you,

Steve

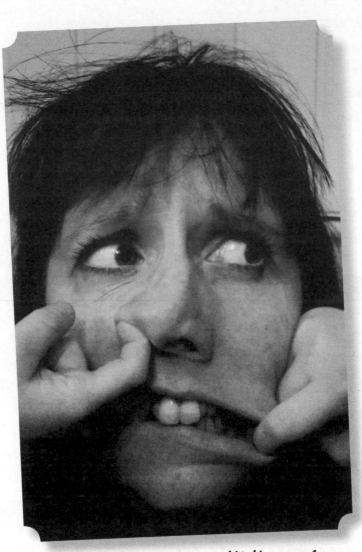

I never did fit in with the mums
who talked about their kids like
trophies. I'm sure Amy is great
at mathematics; my child can
make fart noises with his armpit.
Proud.

You flip the bird behind their backs too?

The motherfucker about motherhood

> *'I want to sit with the mums who laugh at the stupid shit and invite each other round their houses knowing there is a high chance of a skid mark in the toilet but no one really cares because someone brought the cakes.'*

I want to find the mums who are smiling on the outside but broken on the inside. I want the lonely ones who sob in their car at the idea of having to walk into the playground. I want the ones who feel they don't fit in. I'm not secretly a narcissist who likes to sit and watch women cry, but I want them to know they do fit in, we all fit in – it's just about being in a group where you actually belong, where you don't have to try to be something you're not. I want to find them, hang with them and make the dirty jokes because I used to be them: too scared to make eye contact, and constantly overanalysing what I said to make sure I looked like the mum they all expected me to be. Jesus, it's exhausting isn't it?!?! All for the ten-minute pick-up and drop-off. Why do we need to be that fucking petrified over those people?

So this being a mum thing is a bit of a shitshow and, like a deer caught in the headlights, at every single new milestone you put on your best attempt at fart acting and hope you're not scarring the kids – or scaring them – when they realise that you literally have no fucking clue what you're doing. That whole 'they don't write a manual' couldn't be more relevant and you truly understand that now. All this 'it'll come naturally' bullshit means nothing. Because when you have a snotty-nosed four-year-old projectile vomiting at a wall (because they're always incapable of actually getting to the toilet) and you're pretty sure you should be comforting them, deep down you're more worried they're going to pass on whatever skank-ridden cesspit is raging in their body – and you absolutely don't want the shit and spews. Truth be told, being a mother is loving them so much while feeling beyond excited that you have less than an hour to go before they can go to bed.

I don't look like other mums. I mean, I look present-able, I can throw on a lovely scarf, a bit of lippy and look rather wonderful, but I really don't give a shit about how much better my kids are than yours. I just don't, and I'm sorry because I know you love to talk the ins and out of a duck's arse over your child's ability to wipe their own scrotum. I want to talk about sex, I want to talk about how big we think that guy's dick is that just walked past and I want to laugh in the dirtiest of ways so it makes people turn and stare. Why? Because I live and breathe motherhood. I sit and look through photos of my kids, Steve and I talk about them all the time because we adore them, but they aren't my entire life and that isn't a bad thing.

I want to sit with the mums who laugh at the stupid shit and invite each other round their houses knowing there is a high chance of a skid mark in the toilet but no one really cares because someone brought the cakes. I want to be around the mums who laugh when I call my kids pricks, because they get it and it's not that we hate them but that we all share the same understanding – they're hard work and this whole being a mum thing is a lot tougher than we thought.

I tried so hard to fit into circles; once those early months of motherhood support groups began to peter out I was left with the daunting world of toddler groups – where mums constantly close ranks on you whenever you try to initiate conversation – and then the playground groups where I just wanted a couple of friends to talk to. I realised after a while that actu-ally trying so hard isn't worth it if you can't trust the people you surround yourself with. There was always one mum who made passive-aggressive comments, and I was never sure if she hated even the sound of me breathing or was just permanently on her period whenever I was around. I just stopped trying one day, and the biggest surprise in doing so was watching the supposed friends I had collected along the way no longer making that effort – those text messages and personal invites just stopped. I quickly realised they were never friends, but passing moments in my life. I learnt to enjoy my own company as I waited for my children in the playground. I took the new stance of standing alone and revelled in the lack of drama that surrounded my own personal space.

I thought that I would feel lonely, but actually it just felt easy, because I didn't want to be with the superficial clichés. I'd had enough playground drama when I was a kid and, while some thrive on it, I personally find it makes me more anxious. Do you remember when it was your turn to take a piss and you worried what they might be saying when you left the room? Those are the mum friends no one needs.

I found it didn't take long after taking a step back from the witches' cauldron for me to realise how judgemental I'd become of others (*it's invisible, but take a moment to look around at the circle of mums who speak in low voices with wayward eyes at everyone walking past*). I realised I had high expectations of what I felt other mums should be doing and I didn't like that person. While I can sit here and pretend I was all Mrs Chilled and Easy-Going, there have been many moments in my life where I have been anything but. This space wasn't my happy place, and actually all of a sudden I could see much more clearly. These people, they thrive on believing they work harder, have it tougher, they could do it better, the list goes on, but in short they have their heads up their own arses so much I wonder if they see daylight!?

Who can go through life and say they have never fucked up? If that person exists I don't want to meet them, because they must be full of shit. We all say things we regret, we all do things that hurt others, and sometimes no amount of 'I'm sorry' makes up for that. The most important thing I have taken from life, from being a mum, being on the inside and outside of the exclusive groups in the nursery line-up, the Friday morning toddler group and the playground, is to learn from all the times I did something that probably could have been considered a dick move. Whether that be passing comment about something that quite honestly didn't concern me, or assuming I knew what was going on behind closed doors and then discussing it like a total nasty hag with other people. I can hold my hand up and say I have been that person, and I can now put my hand on my heart and say I have realised what a toxic, insanely negative place that is to be. I see so many people who still haven't learnt this, and, while I feel sorry for them, I'm mainly just relieved to not be part of it any more. I have an opinion; I've just learnt when and where it is needed.

I can't blame others because I am responsible for my own thoughts and what comes out of my mouth. It is so much easier to say the reason you behaved a certain way was because of someone else, but that is only ever to lessen the burden of your own guilt, and deep down you know you are to blame for being that much of a judgemental bitch. I think going through depression with Toby truly taught me to try to make fewer assumptions about people and to understand you don't know a fucking thing about that person until you have walked in their shoes.

Sometimes you are going to meet people, you're going to get to know them, and you're going to realise you don't agree with who they are and what they do – that's okay! Everyone else can think they are the bee's knees, but inwardly you will begin to smell something that resembles a festering turd. That gut instinct is often good to follow.

I am often given the stink eye by other mums in the playground, and nine years ago that would have bothered me. The unrest of knowing someone didn't like me without knowing who I was would have sent me over the edge. Now, I just don't give a shit. Those are the people I avoid like a diarrhoea bug without fear of what they might be saying. I dick about in the playground with my children, I hug them, high-five them and I pay no attention to onlooking eyes because I now like to think at least I am giving them something good to talk about.

We won't ever escape judgement; it's the basic human need most people have. They think they could do it differently; they believe they are better at it. Well, crack on love, if you want to spend four hours making a homemade soup with oven-baked bread and a chocolate muffin for afters with hidden veg I'm happy for you, but I have frozen fish fingers and chips, and I can guarantee my children will still go to bed with full tummies. I'm quite happy with 'everything in moderation', which also includes a cheeky drive-thru every so often when I absolutely can't be fucked to cook.

> *'I'm sick of the conversation about part-time parents being lazy, full-time mums not loving their kids and stay-at-home parents not having a grip on reality.'*

So, you're going to be judged for how you feed your kids. Don't forget that bedtime is up for debate too, and let's not forget how much screen time you give them. The ticking time bomb before you explode into a million pieces of panic because everyone is chipping in with what you should and shouldn't do, whether it be the silent cast of a look as you give your kid a tablet at the dinner table in the restaurant or the outspoken opinions that show they think you could be doing it better. Then there is the age-old debate of what level of work people deem acceptable?? Now, isn't that a fun one!

Over nine years of working part-time I have constantly heard the phrase 'so you just work *part-time*' – sometimes weekly – and would you like to know what I say inwardly every time I hear it? I simply say to myself: 'Fuck you.'

Why? Because there is this idea that me working part-time means I get to sit at home giving myself pedicures and having lunch with friends, but the reality is I haven't shaved my bikini line since 2017, let alone painted my toenails.

I'll tell you what the rest of my week consists of – it's leaving the house by 8.15 while trying to detach two feral children from each other who are deciding to have a WWE match in the middle of my overgrown front garden. It's getting in the car and constantly reassuring my naturally anxious little boy with all the reasons he will enjoy school and telling the other child to stop screaming.

By the time it's reached 9am I've fed and dressed two humans, I've mediated the fight over who gets to open the door while mentally trying to remember who was allowed to open the front door the day before (SERIOUSLY BOYS, IT'S A FUCKING DOOR), I've physically thrown one child over my shoulder to get him into the car while calling every single male relative's name until I reach the correct one and tell the other child to get in the (fucking) car and put his (fucking) seatbelt on.

I then have the rest of the day to contend with toddler sessions where I hope my kid isn't the arsehole of the group and lunches that consist of a Babybel and 20 chocolate digestives staggered at varying points during what would be considered 'a lunch time' because I'm in total denial about my sugar dependency. Sometimes I leave the house at 8am and I don't walk back through until 4.30pm, and I then have to wrangle two angry bears into a bath because they smell like testicles and old cheese. By the time my wingman walks through the door I'm quite literally like a human slip 'n' slide of sweat.

The idea that any parent who works part-time or stays at home has it easy is laughable, because it's hard as fuck. While we're trying to keep the little bastards alive, there is an entire house to try to make look less like a crack den and more like a home. That all takes time away from the kids who give each other flying teabags every moment you walk away from them.

Yes, we chose this. Yes, we wouldn't change it. Yes, we understand we don't work as much as you, but that also means we don't get paid the same as you. I'm sick of the conversation about part-time parents being lazy, full-time mums not loving their kids and stay-at-home parents not having a grip on reality. Whatever we've given up to make this life work for us doesn't make it easy; it also doesn't make anything about our lives up for debate.

Why is it the man is entitled to his career when a baby is born but the woman is expected to stand down and wait until her children are 19 and she's menopausal before she gets to pick that dream back up and run with it? Women are constantly questioned about how often they're home for their children, and yet men are hailed heroes when they provide for their family. It truly doesn't matter what we choose to do as women; once we have children there is an almost impossibly thin line to live by that takes you from nailing motherhood to failing. So, next time you think to tell us how easy we have it, remember your opinion is as needed as a yeast infection.

> *'Motherhood isn't a race – you won't get*
> *a half-time orange and no one is going to*
> *give you a medal.'*

Motherhood is a minefield of navigating through endless piles of shit. Sometimes it is actual shit, which rolled out of a nappy as you were about to go on the school run and then the dog ate it. Nothing is going to prepare you for the stress, the expectation from others or the way that makes you feel. Whether you stay at home, work two days a week or have a massive career that takes you all around the world – with vegetable-loving kids or the fish finger wanker brigade – just remember that what it all really boils down to is that it has absolutely fuck all to do with anyone else. Motherhood isn't a race – you won't get a half-time orange and no one is going to give you a medal, not even the playground wanky witches when you make it into school on time. No one is getting out of this alive, so just surround yourself with the women who like wine brunches, heavy carbs and can make the old lady on the next table over blush with stories of piles, poo and periods.

I've been lucky enough to meet those people, just a handful. We aren't looking for endless friendships where we go on family holidays, but we share the fact we don't want the drama that goes with the playground. We stand together in comfortable silence, until the appropriate moment arrives where we say to each other, 'the kids are doing my fucking head in', and we just laugh. The blissful simplicity of knowing we don't need to worry about who is saying what about someone else and whether our kids are better than the others. We rejoice in knowing we love and hate our children equally. Now that is my kind of mum group!

> *'We are their emotional punchbags, the shoulder to cry on, the doctor, the night nurse, the counsellor, the mediator, the friend, the enemy, the stability, the rainy day playdate, sun cream-smothering, anxiety-ridden, lifelong guardian who never, ever stops loving them. It doesn't matter what they do to us; we keep going back for more because that love is something you can't measure.'*

I've never been the mum who loved arts and crafts, never been that great at remembering the school calendar events and I've never been that amazing at remembering to walk away when all of it gets too much. Being a 'good mum' isn't possible, because actually no one nails everything, even Sally Sunshine who doesn't mind her kids making a mess while always having a pristine home.

At times I've wondered: what am I even doing?? How am I doing it? Because it all feels wrong. I think that's normal? If not, someone book me a psych consult because I feel it regularly and I hate it. I worry about how they will see me in the future – will they look back and say I didn't do enough or I wasn't there enough? A bit like Ebenezer Scrooge, I need the ghost of Christmas past and future to pop in and let me know where I need to scrub up on my parenting skills, because sometimes I just want reassurance that no one can give me.

I have two children who are totally different to each other. How is that? They have been brought up the same, and yet they tick differently. That means, as a parent, you have to constantly change the person you are to fit around them. It's exhausting and some days I just don't want to. Not even a little bit. I feel sick of listening to the tantrums, the fighting, and I am even pissed off with the sound of my own voice repeatedly telling them to stop. Why? I just want them to listen to me! I just need them to realise that being a mother means I spend this much of my life pissed off with them for not doing as they're told or making sure they get one last elbow in as I tell them to stop fighting. I sometimes wonder who my neighbours hate more – me, or them? We all scream equally as loud, just theirs is at a new level of high-pitched and is fucking annoying.

Every single parent will have multiple moments of shame, embarrassment and regret, but because they feel so shameful it makes those moments even harder to admit to. Today's society demands it all: the perfectly behaved children, the wonderful home, the full-time job and the stay-at-home parenting, the active social life while remembering to sign your kids up to every single sporting activity the local leisure centre offers, making sure you take the perfectly filtered photo of your child to post on social media so that you can boast about how wonderful they are, as they headlock another kid when you're not looking, and do not forget to keep on top of those waxing appointments where you allow another woman to tickle your gooch with hot wax in the name of fitting into the impossible stereotype that is being an adult in this highly pressured life we all find ourselves in.

Well, sadly, I am going to break it all down to one simple point: we're all the shit mums, but not a lot of us like to admit it. Whether you're making the cake sale bakes or buying them from the Co-op, if you have the child who loves to go food shopping or the one who sits in the trolley and throws everything you put in on the floor, whether they like to sleep or not, and whether you keep the perfect house or not, there will be something in your life, my life and the next Prissy Pamela's life that sucks arse, that makes us carry Mum Guilt, that makes us worry we're not enough. We can all sit and overthink the fucking lot, but all the while we do, just remember there is one or even several little people of varying ages just looking at you, thinking nothing else but: 'Wow, I love you so much!' (Until they're teenagers and then they're just thinking what a cunt you are.)

That's the truth of owning a baby, toddler, pre-schooler, preteen, teen and beyond. It's like being responsible for an angry caged bear that doesn't like to be looked in the eye. You have to love your children with all of your heart; it's basic human survival, because if we didn't I'm absolutely sure we would all drop them at the side of the road and drive off, as sometimes hearing them scream for four fucking hours on end about the fact we haven't yet arrived at our destination is enough to make you sew your own vagina up and promise your-self you'll never have sex again.

It's a pleasure to watch my children grow. Yes, it's incredibly hard, tiring and thankless, but somehow it doesn't ever get so much you just walk away. We are their emotional punchbags, the shoulder to cry on, the doctor, the night nurse, the counsellor, the mediator, the friend, the enemy, the stability, the rainy day play-date, sun cream-smothering, anxiety-ridden, lifelong guardian who never, ever stops loving them. It doesn't matter what they do to us; we keep going back for more because that love is something you can't measure.

It truly is a testament to the strength we have as mothers to constantly take on the shit our kids throw at us. I believe they are not only volatile, but physically and mentally abusive, because they will kick, punch, bite and call you every single name under the sun, and yet we never ever drive them to the gypsies and tell them to take the kid away. What an amazingly fucking awesome and incredibly horrific bond we have with these womb sharers we love so dearly.

Dear Judgey Mum,

I see you, looking at me, as I look back at you. I know
what you're thinking as you put your head down and
keep on walking. You think no doubt you could do it
better, or how I have no control over my children.

Maybe you think something different, but you
know what, in this moment – when I feel so utterly
alone in my life – that look is enough to send me
over the edge. It's enough to make me believe that
maybe I am getting it wrong. I bet you didn't realise
that one casual look over your shoulder as you
pass by could hold that much power? I didn't think
it could until I saw it with my own eyes and felt it
within my own skin.

It could be that you feel awkward; it could be
you feel sorry for me; it could be that you're just
wishing my little boy would stop screaming because
it's annoying. I agree, it is fucking annoying, but you
are only seeing one version of it. I have seen every
single one of them and I can assure you they are
wearing thin, big time!

I have tried the hug it out route; trust me, ten
minutes in and as soon as I try to get back up
they're back to it again, screaming, hitting and
slapping in frustration. They're going through
something right now and as their mum I am along

for the ride, one I wish would end soon. But you aren't asking so you don't know this, you just assume you know what's going on.

That assumption is sometimes the reason I get in my car and cry, because all I ever wanted was someone to place their hand on my shoulder and say, 'Don't worry, I've been there too, and I really hope your day gets better.' Have you ever done this before? I have! Guess what, the mum is always just grateful – not because she thought she was the only one who has a tantrumming child, but because she's so glad someone has acknowledged that this is hard and that she isn't actually doing anything wrong.

You get this, I know you do, but the difference is perhaps that those days are behind you because your children are older and so your recollection is a little vaguer than it used to be. You don't often remember the bad bits in life. We never do, because our brains are so good at filtering out the bad shit. So please just once take yourself back to this time where you were me and remember how it felt. It was hard, tiring and, a lot of the time, lonely. Take yourself back to that woman, then next time you want to shoot me that look, instead just say, 'It's alright, you're doing great.' I will need to hear it, and even coming from a stranger in the street your help and support will continue to build me up.

Those tiny positive encounters stay with us far longer than you might realise, much like those looks. They feel fleeting to you because by the time you are out of earshot those thoughts about me and my son disappear, but they don't for me. They stay with me and they haunt me far longer than they should. I am trying my best and I really want you to understand that. I am trying so hard. I am not shouting, I am not scaring anyone, but I am trying to get to the car, shop, home, wherever it is, with someone who is pushing every single button I have in my body, and under most circumstances I would snap and lose my shit, but I can't because not only are strangers' stares enough to make me question everything I am doing in my life but I also know losing my shit won't solve the problem, so I inwardly count to ten until this incredibly difficult moment is over.

Be sure to look long and hard in the mirror the next time you think about turning your nose up at us, and remind yourself of all the times you haven't been the perfect parent or when your children have pushed you to the limit. Then kindly please go shove your stares up your arse.

All the best,

All us mums hanging by a thread

Rules of the playground

- Absolutely be prepared for Pushy Pamela! Her kids shit gold bars while reciting fluent German and playing the violin. Yes, she is fucking annoying!
- There is always going to be that one teacher that resembles Miss Trunchbull and you're just going to have to hope she doesn't shotput your kid on the sports field.
- The bitching, back-stabbing, secret kissing of someone else's man, whispers on loose lips and finger-pointing – and I ain't even talking about the kids! I shit you not, that playground is a fucking minefield.
- You are going to find yourself stuck within circles that start to resemble witches around a cauldron and you're going to start stirring the pot too. STEP THE FUCK BACK; TUCK AND ROLL OUT OF THERE. Do not become that mum.
- You are going to be expected to remember the bake sale, harvest festival, non-uniform day, World Book Day, dress-like-an-alien Friday, the disco and the sweets on your kids' birthdays. All of your efforts will be silently judged. I like to go with the 'I just bought this from ASDA and nearly missed the school bell' kind of look.

✳ Dickhead Debbie is going to openly invite everyone from your circle of friends back to her house and she's going to leave you out. Don't go home and cry; be sure to find better friends to stand with.

✳ The PTA doesn't appreciate descriptive words like arsehole and bastard when describing your children … That was an awkward 40 minutes of my life I'll never get back.

✳ Really don't worry about that time you forgot to do the homework. Turns out fuckloads of us forget, sometimes weekly. Actually some of us NEVER do it. Don't tell the teacher I told you that.

✳ It's going to be your kid that has the half-masts because you refuse to buy new trousers eight weeks before the end of term. Yes, you're a cheap bitch but you've got a point.

✳ Yes, you'll take them out of school for a reasonably priced holiday and you'll be labelled the Reckless Mum. High-motherfucking-five to you for giving your child an experience no school could ever provide.

✳ There is always going to be that skittish mum who lost the kid's homework, looks like she's not washed in days and awkwardly stands alone like she's either about to shit herself or vomit. Strong chance that mum is me. Go over and say, 'Hello'; I promise she isn't a dick.

Just keep smiling long enough for them to believe you aren't batshit crazy, while repeatedly telling yourself how batshit crazy you feel.

10

When everything goes black

Mental health and survival

> *'The next time you see that red carpet rolled out for the A-lister who talks so openly about their struggle with life and how life now looks like one endless session of bleached arseholes and pina coladas, just remember it takes a team of people to keep them afloat.'*

Somehow being mentally unwell is socially unacceptable. Like, it's not sexy to use the tagline #depressed. We have fallen short in life. We accuse people who are depressed, anxious or self-harming of attention seeking, and the person who says they're going to kill themselves is a drama queen, and not in fact someone desperately crying out for help. What the fuck? I mean, seriously. The reality is, every single person will be touched by mental health in some capacity in their lifetime, whether it is someone they love who is suffering or they themselves falling into the black pit of despair. We make too many assumptions and don't think to ask enough questions about whether someone's okay and how we can help them. We don't try hard enough to understand, because the reality of mental health is that it's vast and complex.

I think mental health can actually be glamorised because we only ever see the end product, after the smelly stage where nothing is washed, hair is greasy and vaginas are raging, and the helpless feeling of completely losing a grip on life is nothing but a distant memory. We see this beautiful thing emerge ready to speak openly about the trauma they have had to live through and they, in turn, then get the attention, the affirmation for being brave and courageous. We look up to them when they finally shine with health and freshly washed armpits, and yet we lacked that admiration when they were at their worst.

I've been through a lot. I have self-harmed and I have skipped meals. I have looked at my tiny frame and told myself I am too fat. I have been that person who, on many occasions, has been so anxious she has felt like she was about to have a heart attack. I know that depression can be glamorised, because I see people looking up to me on social media like some kind of shining beacon of hope that someday they might be just like me, flaps flying, happy and fixed.

The reality is I'm not fixed. Neither is the next person. Nor the massive huge famous movie star who talks about their journey as you crave their style, sass and money – they are carrying those scars, too. There is a good reason psychologists and therapists are always rammed with clients, because there is no quick fix for mental health. It's a bit like having a gym membership – unless you keep pedalling and stepping on that treadmill you are going to lose the stamina to keep on top of this shit you had thought you would never lose again. The less work you put in the less likely you'll feel strong enough to manage it.

So, the next time you see that red carpet rolled out for the A-lister who talks so openly about their struggle with life and how life now looks like one endless session of bleached arseholes and pina coladas, just remember it takes a team of people to keep them afloat. Only your team isn't an on-site therapist, chef, personal trainer, fucking dog whisperer and a panpipes acoustic version of Whitney Houston's 'I Will Always Love You'. Your team is the mum who rings every morning just to check you're doing alright. The best mate who pops in with that bar of chocolate. It's the kids who come running in every morning even though you wish they'd fuck off. But that team of people love you beyond measure, and they aren't there for a pay cheque; they're there because everything about you makes them want to make you happy again. They aren't often going to get it right, that chocolate bar isn't fixing shit, but the point is they are trying so hard, and they aren't going anywhere. In amongst the drama, they're just sitting there patiently waiting with you. These people are the best kind because they don't need to get it to support you.

In our darkest moments we can feel so horribly lonely and it's not until we look back that we truly see the people in the darkness with us, holding our hand, trying so hard to understand it while desperately trying to find a way out with you. Never feel like you are alone, because unfortunately, as you read this right now, there are so many people engulfed, just like you, barely putting one foot in front of the other and wondering how much longer they can take the misery surrounding the massive umbrella that is mental health.

> *'It often hits like a massive tonne of bricks and I sit around the chaos of my mind wondering how the fuck I could go mental that quickly!'*

For me, my mental health never declines slowly. There is no halfway slap on the arse to say, 'Hey sista, things look like they're getting messy. You better do something about this shitshow.' No, it often hits like a massive tonne of bricks and I sit around the chaos of my mind wondering how the fuck I could go mental that quickly! Either I am fuck awful at reading the telltale signs until it's too late, or I totally ignore every single one of the bastards because I keep telling myself it'll be alright in the morning. The longstanding bitch in my life is the anxiety, because that just kicks you right in the hole, doesn't it?? Like, 'Hey, we have five minutes spare here; let's just squeeze in a little bout of self-loathing. Why the fuck not!' I used to fear alone time, where I had no one to see or talk to. Being in my own company was a negative, because then all I'd be left with was my own thoughts and soon enough I'd be working out all the grimy details of how and where I was going wrong.

Up until giving birth to Toby, I had always thought, in my ignorance, that anxiety looked like a person breathing into a paper bag, rocking in a corner, who never left the house. I remember one morning my sister ringing me and saying, 'Laura, I've been googling it' – good old Google – 'and I think you have something called post-natal anxiety.' It was like something clicked in my body and I realised I had lived with anxiety nearly all my life. I'd never been told; it had never been explained to me – it all came down to my worried sister trying to figure out what the fuck was wrong with me. Google confirmed that all those irrational feelings I had with Elliott, the lack of sleep with both kids … it all boiled down to anxiety. My anxiety was a total bitch (still is) and has ruled every single moment of my life.

I felt empowered by this new-found knowledge because it explained a lot, but it also meant I now knew and I couldn't forget the fact: this heavy pain in my chest, the heart palpitations, the excuses to avoid meeting people and overthinking every single aspect of my life, it had a name and its name was general anxiety disorder. Blissfully unaware beforehand, I'd assumed everyone felt like I did; why would you question something you've never not known about???

I didn't expect anxiety to be so frustrating. You know deep down you don't need to be worrying about the thing that is circling around your mind, and yet it completely consumes you. You can't sleep and you become obsessed. I have health anxiety, which in short means if you even so much as let a wet fart go in front of me I will automatically assume you have diarrhoea and that you are going to give it to me. It has never stopped me being near people; there's nothing a well-timed smile and a heavy squirt of antibac won't fix. But if only that were the end of it.

I will allow the appropriate incubation period of whatever ailment I've convinced myself you have before declaring myself disease-free, and only then can I unclench the taut muscles in my arse, knowing I'm not going to die from 'dysentery' that just was a wet fucking fart. If that sounds fun, then I can assure you: it's not. Yet can you imagine verbalising that? 'Please can you tell me the density, consistency and odour of that fart? Do you believe it leaked anal juices? Or was it more of an unfortunate case of crack sweat meeting your arse trumpet?' Yeah, you can't, but I want to! Because it would then save me the heartache of 48 hours constantly telling myself I am on the cusp of something so awful I might not make it out alive.

It is actually exhausting. How can your brain running at a million miles per hour not be debilitating? I believe I have been absolutely emotionally drained by it for the best part of 20 years.

Steve has asked me in the past, 'What are you thinking right now?', to which I reply, 'Which sentence? Because the general conversation sounds a lot like hhhhm-mmmm.' There are so many thoughts going through my head all at once that I can't really pin down the exact thing I might be thinking. I am generally thinking about a million things, which is actually less about anxiety and more just being a woman, because I'm pretty sure the only things that cross Steve's mind are boobs, when he can go for a poo and getting angry when he gets 'Baby Shark' stuck in his head.

> *'The easiest thing to believe is that nothing can fix the problem. Well, how the chuffing hell will you ever know if you don't just give it a go?'*

The most common fact about when we are at our worst is we do not talk. To anyone. We bury it good and proper, because it feels a lot like opening Pandora's box – when you're at your most vulnerable you just don't know what'll burst out if you dare to take a peek. I close off completely. I don't like anyone to know anything about me. I give simple answers and I gloss over fucking everything relating to anything about my day-to-day life.

In fact, I have found dealing with my own shit to be too hard, too painful. Instead, I focus on making others happy, I comfort them in their time of need, I reassure them into believing they can get through it. On the surface it seems lovely, sweet and kind, which I guess it is, but I can't help feeling it's partly selfish because helping others alleviates that heavy weight within my own mind. I have always said that a smile hides a million heartaches and deceives the smartest of people, because if used in the right moment you can go through

life completely unidentified as the person who is clinging on to the cliff edge for dear life. By diving head first
into someone else's heartache I find the overall angst I
feel inside slightly lifted, almost like 'Thank fuck it's not
just me', while keeping my own floodgates firmly shut
because there is always only ever room for one crisis at
a time. Only problem is, I never make time for my own
crisis until it's too late and I am thrust in to deal with it
in the ugliest of ways.

I am not the biggest fan of letting people in when I'm
in the thick of it. I can be incredibly private because I
don't have the mental capacity to deal with the questions of whether I am feeling better ... why I think it has
happened. I don't want the questions; I just want to be
left alone to deal with my anguish. When I say I'm not
the biggest fan I mean even the thought of it gives me
squeaky bum syndrome. I like to make sure everyone
else is unravelling first.

I look back at the teenage girl who got caught cutting
her arms in the bath and I wish she'd gotten the help
she needed back then, rather than trying to find sneak-
ier ways to do it without being caught. I think there
would have been a strong chance of a different adulthood if I had addressed my problems back then – my
horrific insecurities about myself and tragic self-loathing. I wish there had been someone who said, 'Hey let's
talk!' And just listened without making assumptions or
jumping to conclusions on my behalf. Back in the 1990s

there wasn't the knowledge or understanding of things like that, and it meant so many people felt incredibly isolated, not to mention way too petrified to speak out, because the chances were you would be labelled a freak, and, considering I had buck teeth, frizzy hair and freckles, this bitch really didn't need another name to be added to her extensive list of insults.

If someone had fallen over, cracked their head open, cried, and the people in the street stopped and told them they were wrong for crying over it, what would you do? High-five the whangers for abusing that person for their pain? Or take your shoe off and clout the fuckers over the head for being such douchebags? I am hoping there is a majority vote for the clouting shoe.

It comes down to that very same thing with mental health – when someone makes you question your own feelings, when they insist your sadness and struggles are wrong, it's time to think about why you allow someone that negative to dominate your thought processes. The next time you are left doubting what is going on in the inside by someone on the outside, just remember the only person in control of your own destiny is you. Take it with both hands and guide it in the direction you need it to go to find that self-contentment and happiness. Whether that be antidepressants, cognitive behavioural therapy, a psychologist, acupuncture or a weekend retreat, for the love of God just do it for you and no one else.

I have spent so much of my life looking to others to validate my own feelings. Like, do you think I am okay? If you say yes, then cool, it must be true. It makes life easier and for a while it also fixes the problems in your own head: 'Well, Uncle Jeremy said I looked well put-together and he is really fucking old so he must know.' But, I mean, it raises the question how the fuck I have managed to get this far in life when I've been relying on others to tell me how I'm meant to be feeling. It's hardly a successful tool for making smart choices for your own happiness.

It isn't okay to brush these things under the carpet, but the reality of facing those feelings is so scary and unknown. How do you begin to unravel the shitmess that is your scrambled brain? Do you have to take it to your grave? Or do you find the person who can gently sit you down and slowly unpack each heavy box that weighs your mind down? Darling, you are going to cry. Fuck my life, you will hurt and shit the bed, you will be petrified, but take a moment and imagine me stood in front of you right now. If I was carrying those boxes that occupy the space in your mind – and you know what they feel like to live with – what would you tell me? Thank fuck, it's your problem now; I'm off to the pub? Or would you help me to deal with those demons?

Asking for help isn't a weakness; it's actually a sign of strength. You're at that point where you're willing to change things up a bit, inject a little spark into your life, and this will in turn become one of your greatest achievements. I think the easiest thing to believe is that nothing can fix the problem. Well, how the chuffing hell will you ever know if you don't just give it a go?

Mental health is incredibly lonely, and, no matter how many times you go through it, that doesn't ever change. You get better and tell not just yourself but everyone else around how it'll be different next time because you will speak up, but you don't because it's so hard. To admit there is a problem is usually the hardest part, but once you do this then you can finally begin to find the road to recovery.

> *'By being open and honest on Knee Deep In Life, I have gained comfort in knowing I'm so far from being alone.'*

Sometimes I can wake up and feel the day is too much. Generally, it will happen when the day before was a really great, blissfully happy one. It's like all my endorphins were sucked out with the mood hoover as I went to bed and fell into the next day. My mood hasn't ever truly stabilised since having Toby – something I have at times found hard to admit, because you don't want to be that person still carrying around the baggage from four years ago. I can pretend this isn't the case, but for whose benefit would that be? To lead you to believe I'm fixed? So that you can think that not only have I got my shit together, but that I own it too?? I see first-hand how these toxic false truths leave people feeling. I find myself looking at people in the spotlight and hoping they'll be honest about how life isn't this perfect, endless magazine cover, but they never do, which then on my bad days leads me to believe it truly is just me getting it wrong. Well, let me tell you, we are all in this together.

I have found writing to be my best therapy. By being open and honest on Knee Deep In Life, I have gained comfort in knowing I'm so far from being alone. I wish I had spoken up sooner, I wish I had been more honest with those around me – the 'I wishes' are as long as this book – but I can't spend the rest of my life reliving them because then I'd waste another lifetime on moments I can't change.

I don't feel like the reject any more. I spoke my mind and waited to see who clapped back – and it was such a wonderful moment because when I'd only dared hope for a single clap in the audience, instead I was deafened by the sound that came back.

Who's that trip-trapping over my bridge?

Well, ain't that a bitch! Turns out not everyone likes me! They come with their skanky hooves and they try to tear me down. Why? Shits and giggles? Insecure? Just coz? Who knows. I remember when I first started my blog and I mentioned *whispers* poo. Some random middle-aged woman took offence and called me vulgar. I made out I didn't care, but fuck I did. I wanted it to not bother me, and yet there I was, trying to find a new and interesting word for shit.

I've realised, though, that the idea that we can please everyone in life is wonderful, but it's not achievable. To be honest, I'm quite happy skidding my way through life, dragging along the people who are in for the ride too, and letting go of the people who believe their bumhole opinion matters to me. I shit you not.

The abuse I receive online has only given me a thicker skin with which to laugh it off. They must be missing something in their lives, whether that's a little clit stimulation or an extra hug every now and then. The number of women who troll me was a big surprise. Men make stupid comments like

'nice tits' or 'you ugly munt!' but they're one-liners,
throwaway comments, which are (no offence, lads)
something a 12-year-old boy would say. But women
pull it out the bag big time, and they know how to
make it hurt. They send DMs and call me out for
being a bad mum. They write nasty comments. They
vent. This letter is for them.

Dear Trolly,

How are you doing? Hang on, don't answer
that, I don't give a shit. Why? Because not
once did you ask how I was before you
chose to make assumptions about who I am
and what I do. Never did you contemplate
the mental health of others when you
tore them a new one online in your bid to
activate your lifetime membership of Uptight
Arseholes R US.

I understand your need to find the ugly
in our lives – you like to dig deep – but, quite
frankly, I'm pretty sure we wouldn't have
to dig too deep to see that your shit stinks
too. You love to make others weak and so I
surmise that it must have a lot to do with
your own inner peace.

Babe, I have just one question for you. And
it's an important one so please, just listen up!
When was the last time you had an orgasm?

It's been a while, hasn't it? You poor fucker;
go buy a dildo, be sure to set it to max and
don't stop until you feel that stick up your
arse slowly start to dislodge. I'm unsure if you
realise but I'll just officially clarify this for all
you bitches at the back who didn't hear me
the first time – this is me and I literally give
zero fucks what you think about me. I guess
that means all those efforts were wasted,
which I appreciate is a disappointment,
because all you ever want to do is bask in the
misery of others.

I'm sure that if you follow those simple
step – try to relax and I would suggest lying
down during insertion – you'll soon have your
legs straight in the air, resembling a dead
goat screaming with pleasure. You truly don't
need to thank me, because actually my thanks
go to you for reminding me that even on my
darkest days, when I could have been a total
douchebag, I chose to not be you. I chose to
always try to be the person my kids look
up to. One day I know my children will ask
questions over the decisions I've made, for the
person I have chosen to be on the internet,
and I'll proudly say I did it to liberate people
to believe in themselves.

I worry for how your children will look at you, God forbid they ever discover your dirty little secret, as you hide behind the protection of your computer or phone with fake names and faceless photos. We teach children to respect others and to understand the strength in standing up for what we believe in, and the deepest tragedy in the current trolling situation is you're all grown, fully responsible adults, raising the next generation. I worry more for your children than I do mine.

I mean, if you're still reading this and you hate me that's awesome and hilarious. Now go fuck off on your broom and return to society when you've learnt the basic human instinct programmed into most people, which is respect for yourself and common decency for others.

Love and best wishes,

Laura

A little reminder to you ...

My darling, you've been through a lot. You feel tired!
All the time! And the days are just long and empty.
Sometimes it feels like there's no hope, and actually
that's a very lonely place to be. Everyone can be
there helping you, loving you, but when they can't
understand what's going on inside your mind, it can
feel like a losing battle to try to explain yourself.
Here are some things I'd like you to remember:

✳ This road is yours to walk and while it might be
  long you are still on it. Keep stepping forward
  towards the future where you are better.
✳ Your smile. Wow! Your smile makes everyone feel
  good when they see it. Now it's time to make sure
  you smile from the inside out.
✳ Don't read all the negative bullshit that makes
  your anxiety spiral. That isn't your journey. It
  is someone else's; never let it define your own
  recovery.
✳ Let the right people in. The ones who will lie in
  bed with you all day and binge-watch Netflix all
  because they love you enough to be around you;
  and also let them kick your arse when they tell
  you to go wash your vagina.

❉ Those people standing in the wings, always catching you when you fall – you aren't lucky to have them, they are lucky to have you. There is a reason they're still here and it's YOU.

❉ When you look back at this time, it will always hurt, but focus on the strength it gave you, the fight you fought and the life you are now living.

❉ Depression, anxiety, PTSD, bulimia, anorexia, OCD, bipolar ... and the list goes on. The next time you feel alone, remember how huge mental health is, and how you are closer to someone going through the same thing than you think.

❉ Don't be ashamed of your story; it's part of who you are. Always be proud of surviving.

❉ When you feel you have nothing else to give, just remember to be kind to yourself.

Sometimes you have to take a giant leap of faith and hope for the best. You might land on your feet, you might fall flat on your arse – but what a fucking ride it'll be.

The future's bright, the future's knee deep

Dream big – what ya got to lose?

> *Growing up I wanted to be an actress, then I dropped out of performing arts in the first term because I realised that whenever I tried to sing the other students put their fingers in their ears. That was the girl I was back then, so worried about what everyone else thought, rather than the woman who now just sings louder to really piss off the ear pluggers. Back then, I fell into the rhythm of life instead: fell in love, settled down, bought a house, got married, had kids.*

The young me, she yearned for that stable life, but she was also desperate for that career where I became a famous movie star. When I was a teenager who struggled to cope with having to tidy her own room, let alone work hard at her acting skills, which by the way were bordering on piss poor (although I did get a B in drama, something I still ride the coat-tails of 20 years on), I failed to realise that it all takes constant work!

I am pleased success has come to me at a later age. I feel for the young generation – the pressure, the unreal level of responsibility to be an adult long before they're meant to, as the flashing bulbs of cameras constantly go off, waiting for them to fuck up. I would have been the broken Britney if I had found fame at such a young age. Fuck my life, I would have been that poor bitch shaving my head and attacking people with umbrellas.

At the time it didn't feel much like a reassuring relief that I wasn't making it at the thing I also wasn't trying to make it in. I secured a job doing shitty admin two hours away, and was driven there by my dad (he worked there too. That would be taking 'asking for a lift' to a whole new level of taking the piss otherwise). I hated this version of my life; there was no glamour, no ease, it was all a lot of hard work. Real life is a total prick, isn't it?? I remember telling my parents I would move out of home by the time I was 17 and would never come back. I didn't particularly hate it; I just thought living alone would be a piece of piss. There should definitely be lessons in school where they sit kids down and say: 'Look, beyond this point, it's all going to get a little sketchy. You're probably going to wish you could sack off work for six weeks like you've done in school for the last sixteen years of your life, but now you have no fucking choice; there are no long holidays, and soon you will get so excited for a bank holiday you'll think that extra day to do fuck all is like being flown to Paris for the weekend.'

I was a very normal person, living a very normal life, and dreamt of moments where I could succeed. I used to start writing novels for fun, just coz what else do you do on a Saturday night? I would get it into my head I would be the next famous author, or I would decide I was going to become a teacher (before quickly remembering I fucking hate other people's children). I never really knew where to go with it all. Steve got used to my random bursts of desperation where I wanted to do something that would change our lives for ever. Moving to New York was one of them; also running a marathon, long before I had even contemplated even running to the end of the road.

What did I want to do with my life? I was approaching 30 with next to no idea and I felt like a complete failure. I didn't want to just be a mum and wife, and while I felt bad for that never being quite enough, I needed something more. I was older and I was prepared to work for it, but, unless some bastard was willing to sit me down and talk through my objectives, I was pretty sure I would continue to just drift through life believing this was just it.

Then four years ago I was wrapped up in some serious shit-hot mess and I felt like the pit I had fallen into was way too deep to climb out. Why me? Why was everyone else making life look so much easier? How were they managing to make it look glamorous? I thought maybe I'd just stay there for ever, hairy minge, smelly pits and a total lack of lust for life. I absolutely couldn't see a way through. And yet I somehow managed to crawl my way out, slowly, and then I realised I had nothing left to lose.

There were all these amazing people living these amazing lives plaguing my social media, over and over, making me feel like utter shit (which I know was never their intention). So I started to message them to find out how they were doing it, and I was pretty shocked to find it actually wasn't like that. I realised maybe they too were suffering with depression, or their husband had cheated on them, that maybe they were struggling with how demanding being a mum was. But online they just talked about all the good bits about life.

'Oh ... so there are no sunshine and rainbows at the end?? We're all struggling in different ways??? FUCK!' That was an eye-opener, and I began to recognise that I was also that person, putting a rose-tinted view of life out there. I was the wanker with the filtered photos who talked about the lovely bits, because the bad bits made me feel so sad I could cry.

> *'That is how I've ended up in some of the most incredible situations in my life – my blog being one of them – because I haven't always given it enough thought to wonder if it'll fail.'*

I started doing side-by-side photos and exercise videos with Steve in the summer of 2016, just for fun on my own personal page. Friends started saying I should start a blog: 'Give it a go!' I kept brushing them off, like it was an insane idea and no way I could do it. HAHAHA of course I had every fucking intention of doing it. I wanted to be successful and now my unrealised goal to be a famous author was out of the window, I was going to be a famous blogger instead.

By October 2016 I plunged myself into my blog and I started to find the confidence to not care who saw what I said or what I looked like. For the first time in my life I was doing something completely for me. While I always hoped to be a successful, I didn't believe it would ever actually happen to me. Nothing I did was tactical to get ahead in life, I was just doing it because it simply brought me enjoyment. I liked the fact I challenged issues – I had a voice and I wanted to be heard about gender equality, the unrealistic perception everyone had in life about what a woman should look like, and how we were meant to act. I was tired of the yummy mummy preconceived ideas of how we just love our kids all the time and never leave the house without a smile. I wanted to make people laugh, think and feel less alone. The success came as a bit of a surprise even though it was small, maybe 50 followers and then 75 over the space of two months, but seeing new people joining my page gave me confidence to believe I was actually speaking for a lot of women.

I loved this place like it was a third baby. I poured my heart out, sometimes crying as I typed, because I was talking about traumas I was still trying to deal with. I got told a lot in the early days by friends and family that I swore too much, or that I shouldn't do the photos. I felt myself being swayed by their opinion, but not long after I would find myself falling back into the comfortable shoes of being in my underwear because: this was me! I wasn't meant to change for anyone else. So I stood my ground and I began to make the armoured jacket that I now wear to deflect a lot of the idle criticism over what I should or shouldn't be doing as a woman on the internet.

The day my blog went viral I'd received a pair of Spanx in the post. As soon as the parcel hit the mat in our hall, I ran upstairs, taking my clothes off as I went, ignoring the kids as they fought over the TV remote, and opened the package with excitement. Of course, I wanted to record myself trying them on. I haphazardly placed my camera up against a can of dry shampoo and hit record. I tugged, I pulled, I poured with sweat while giving a monologue of how fucking awful it felt, just as they rolled up around my waist to form a thin tyre. I panicked! I shouted for the kids to help me – of course they never fucking came – and I tried to finish the video as calmly as possible while being vaguely aware I was due around my parents' house in 30 minutes for lunch. Even walking hurt; it was so tight wrapped around my waist that my only option was to yank, pull and shunt the Spanx off along with my pants. I sat naked on the end of my son's bed with sweat dripping off me and a slight sigh of relief that I didn't actually die from the Spanx perforating an organ. I didn't edit it, I hit upload and didn't give it much more thought, as I hurriedly tried to get the kids dressed and out the door.

That afternoon, I sat in my parents' conservatory watching the numbers tripling, the shares happening by the thousands, and I felt this anxiety bubble up to the surface that meant I couldn't eat or sleep for days. This is what I wanted deep down; much like that Lotto win, you never think it will happen and then all of a sudden it's no longer a dream but a reality ... and yet I was shitting myself big time. I felt like I was on high alert for a zombie apocalypse, except no one was dying or had come back as the living dead. This was meant to be a good thing! This was meant to be really positive, but I was petrified and, worse than that, I literally had no idea what I was doing. This was a whim! This wasn't calculated and thought out. I'd just placed my phone on the cabinet in my hallway, hit record and then got stuck in Spanx. What the fuck??? I expected a response like a couple new followers and some extra laughs.

I guess that sums up me as a person. I'm an impulsive bitch, I always have been, and so there haven't always been fully thought-out plans for how I would execute the situations I put find myself in. A prime example is when I decided to hang off a door upside down (why the fuck not) for a photo in my underwear (standard evening in my house) and it wasn't until I'd climbed up the ladder, straddled the door and, like the slow motion of a pendulum, it swung closed, that Steve said, 'Laura, have you thought about how you're getting down?' To which I do believe my response was simply, 'Fuck!' No, I hadn't. And so, like something out of a knock-off porno version of *The Matrix*, I found myself with half a tit hanging out of the pants I had turned into a makeshift boob tube (I am so resourceful) being manhandled by my husband, who was desperately trying to make sure I didn't die because there was no way the life insurance would pay out for this sort of accident. I found myself walking up the wall onto the ceiling, with him yelling, 'What the fuck do you think you're doing?!' because in the moment I had forgotten about gravity and genuinely believed I could just walk myself back down the wall. (All that did, in fact, happen is Steve fucked his back. I ran out of ceiling and wall to walk on and fell, from a relatively great height, in the hope he would somehow turn into The Rock and just catch me! I lay on the carpet with friction burn across my thighs and all I had to say to Steve was, 'Please tell me you got the fucking photo.')

That is how I have ended up in some of the most incredible situations in my life – my blog being one of them – because I haven't always given it enough thought to wonder if it'll fail. I'm not saying that's a recipe for success, because, well, let's be honest, being the stupid twat who hangs from a door upside down, all for a cheap laugh, isn't the key to ultimate happiness and peace within yourself.

> *'I have learnt to accept that the most important thing I can ever give myself is a break.'*

I always dreamt of what life would be like if I ever managed to get through the pearly gates of being a successful blogger. I thought it was this massive party of people high-fiving you and welcoming you in. Well, that was a shocker, because it felt a lot more like a high-five to the face as people closed ranks, and you all of a sudden felt like the only dick at the party who showed up in fancy dress.

That being said, I have had the pleasure of meeting people through my blog who have gone on to become some of my closest friends, who have heavily supported me. If nothing else, that's been a very special gift I didn't expect to find. I have been heavily supported, encouraged and had the pleasure of talking to some people I have looked up to for such a long time. I don't think I can explain how that feels because all this time I honestly saw them as up in the gods of celebrity society, when in actual fact they're just normal people, doing normal everyday stuff. They actually talk to me... and I try to act cool about it every single time. FYI: I never feel cool, and I'm always silently fan girling. I've found a true sisterhood of women, some I've never met, and yet we all share in the same thing and that is to be kind and support each other with no expectations of anything back.

It's been a tougher road than I'd expected and the rose-tinted glasses are well and truly off. The road to self-acceptance can't be found within the hands of other people telling you that you're doing a good job. It has to be within you. Whether it be that manager's job you just got and you think everyone hates you for, or the new friendship where you are desperate to be liked, you need to learn to believe in who you are and that you don't need to change to fit in.

I have been considered very inappropriate and a bit like Marmite, but what a fucking lovable spread I make. I get it and so there have been many times where I have questioned what I do and whether I'm totally getting it wrong, because someone else is more successful, liked more, or they just seem more accepted for who they are as a person. At times that has sucked massive balls, because although my main aim is helping women to find self-acceptance, and to learn to love themselves, deep down aren't we all trying to be liked (unless you're a complete twunt who loves to be a total knob). We aren't always going to get it right for everyone, but I have learnt to accept that the most important thing I can ever give myself is a break.

Why try to fit into places where you didn't belong in the first place? I have tried for so long, and it's exhausting to pretend to care about someone else's shit when in actual fact that person absolutely doesn't care about yours!

Since launching Knee Deep In Life, I have grown massively, and in the process my circle has become tighter. The people who support me have become fiercer – they've had to because you get a lot of shit when you put yourself out there for all to see. I have found that as I've been accepted, my courage has only grown stronger. My hope was always to reach 10,000 followers, I'm not sure why, but at the time it seemed completely unachievable, and so it felt like a massive dream to have that many thousands of women laughing with me and feeling better about themselves because of it. However, it felt like a dream I would work for, even if I probably never got to it.

You know when you fantasise about winning the Lotto? The one where you have genuine conversations about what you'll do with the money. Like, you decide you'll buy the winning ticket in approximately four weeks, by which time you will already have a long-term plan for where all those millions will go. You know the conversation because we all have it, and we all dream it. Well, my blog going big was, for me, like winning the Lotto. I'd talked to Steve about what I would do if it happened while inwardly thinking there wasn't a chance.

I couldn't have begun to anticipate this! This is everything, and I don't understand how I managed to get this far. I sometimes have the worst imposter syndrome because it doesn't feel like I deserve it all. You see all the other people working their arse off, incredible and talented people, and somehow you're the one going viral. I've been asked how I managed to make it happen. What pointers I have. Truth is, I have no fucking idea! How bad is that?!? Yet it is the complete truth – seriously guys, I'm as shocked as you that it's happened, and it's taken me such a long time to feel like I am big enough to fill the even bigger shoes I've found myself in.

I always told Steve that when I hit a certain level of followers I would feel like I had made it. Then I'd hit that level and I'd move the goalposts. I would find a new reason to work harder in the hope of reaching more people. I don't think at any point I've really given myself a break. I always thought arriving here, in this moment, would feel a lot like the finishing line at a marathon, like someone comes running up to you with a hug and a well done.

Just to clarify, they don't. Not sure why I thought that would happen? But it's been harder to accept that this person who does the school run, picks her nose, farts, burps and is very rarely invited out for the evening is now stopped in the street for a photo. I feel my bumhole widen to the size of a donkey's nostril because I literally don't know what I'm meant to say or do. Tap dance?? Do a striptease? I'm praying it's not the striptease because I can guarantee I won't have shaved my vagina for a considerable period of time. It's just not every day people recognise you as you buy tampons in Asda, or as your kids throw massive tantrums in the street. You know, why is this shit still happening to me?? The normal day-to-day. Surely I should have a Bentley, personal shopper and a nanny by now? (Not sure who you have to suck to get that personal shopper, but I'm willing to go deep.)

I think it's a healthy thing to arrive at the destination you worked for only to find you are hungry for more. I love and loathe the fact I am never complacent. Sometimes I wish I could give myself a night off from worrying I will ultimately fuck the whole lot up. Apart from my husband and my children, I have never loved anything this much – the journey it has taken me on and the fact I don't see it as a job; I just completely and utterly love it.

I sometimes wonder if I were standing in front of me, having just met me and listened to the experience I've had, what would I say. Probably: well done! And yet the idea of saying it to myself in the mirror leaves a nasty taste in my mouth and a wiggly feeling in my bum. Like being able to give myself recognition for what I've achieved is somehow shameful. Why do we do that? How can we be that shit at self-reflection when we're more than capable of showering a complete stranger with compliments?

Is this just me? I hope not! I truly hope I'm not the only person who's yet to fulfil all the things she promised herself while already smashing all the hope and dreams she had ever had. The red carpet and medal don't go to anyone, those things are happening because of you, and it's about time we all recognised that and accepted we're the reason for these awesome things.

Let's just learn to give ourselves five minutes every day to write down the things we achieved. They could be the same things every single day:

- Got up
- Took the kids to school

- Made dinner
- Put the kids to bed
- Watched TV

Now why aren't we just taking a moment to recognise these things are an accomplishment? There isn't this massive crash, bang, wallop in life that says 'hey, look, you arrived'; it's a slow burner that changes over time. It is important to note those tiny turning points that lead you to the path that allows good things to happen, whether that be a new relationship, job, a pay rise or a different sexual position that makes you orgasm quicker. Why aren't we noting the journey? I wish I had; I wish I could go back to me the night before my blog went viral and relive whatever my thought process was – no doubt I thought that I wasn't funny enough, good enough or capable of being successful – to gain perspective on how far that person of self-doubt has come in such a short space of time.

In the early days, it was bum-clenchingly scary, and there were so many moments where I wondered if this was even what I wanted. The exposure left me feeling laid bare, and I didn't know that this was how it would feel. People I hadn't spoken to in years were all of a sudden wanting to meet up, and old school friends who never spoke to me were friend requesting me. I can remember meeting with a friend for coffee and telling her how it all made me feel, how this experience didn't feel much like a glorious dream come true, that it felt like an ugly nightmare I couldn't wake up from. I'm just trying to be myself in anything I post, and not trying to be anything I'm not. What if I was only that funny once? What if all these people following me now were expecting that, and I wouldn't ever deliver it again? How could I cope with that level of rejection? Would it just be better to bow out now and stop while it's good?

My friend said, 'The moment it stops being fun, and you can't get back from it what you put in, deactivate the page. You don't owe these people anything, and actually your happiness is more important than anything else.'

Those words kind of hung there for a moment. Just delete it! I could walk away right now and become the faceless woman once more. In that moment I realised how much this place meant to me. That I would need to work through this level of anxiety because I needed Knee Deep In Life more than I had ever realised. This daily therapy session where I talked about anything and everything had become something so important I couldn't ever just drop it and walk away.

My blog becoming so successful has taught me a new level of strength, which is to fight for things I am passion-ate about. I've had posts taken down by the powers that be because they deemed them unacceptable or inappro-priate, mainly because I haven't been scared to use my platform for important things. I've never stopped using my voice to be heard over things like female empowerment, body equality, discrimination, and constantly trying to speak openly about mental health without fear that I might say something wrong.

I never expected my voice to resonate so loudly with others. I never anticipated my stupid photos would help people through their dark days, and I didn't appreciate how many people needed to hear those things until I started saying them. I enjoy pushing the limits of what is socially acceptable because it's about time someone did. We are women who grow hair in annoying places, and sometimes that includes our top lip. We don't always like to shave our armpits and we will quite often turn down sex because we're tired or we just don't want to do it. I love that in saying those things I've been met with thousands of women clapping back, saying, 'Thank you.' Truly, what a moment to arrive in life, when you see on such a huge scale that you aren't alone.

-Laura's Life Lesson - - - - -

Don't wait for the perfect opportunity to chase your dreams, even though the fear of the unknown can be debilitating. You get one hop, skip and a jump on this planet, so be sure to slide into that coffin by the skin of your teeth, knowing you lived it the way you always wanted. Be the person who leaves behind a million memories that make people smile, but most of all be the person who lived your life for you and no one else.

Absolute worst-case scenario, you realise that dream you were chasing isn't as much fun as you thought and that you really fucking hate it. Granted, that might be a bit of a shitter, but at least you can tick it off your bucket list and move on to the next thing!

How could I leave without
reminding you all of the reasons
why you are wonderful, worthy,
beautiful and absolutely capable
of every single thing your heart
desires. This chapter, my beautiful,
is all for you.

Afterword

Hello, you

> 'Be brave and be you. I promise that not
> only is it enough, but that it's all you've
> got, so make it count.'

So, we're at the end. I have one last chance to tell you
something huge – YOU ARE AMAZING. You are imperfect; life isn't how you had planned it and you constantly
feel like someone else could be and is doing better. The
shitty reality is, they aren't – not even remotely close –
but they're doing a good enough job of making it look
easy. I've learnt that houses don't stay clean, kids are
never grateful, work isn't ever easy and self-doubt is the
biggest prick of all. You aren't always going to want to
bang throughout the night like a sex-crazed teenager,
because the truth is none of us do.

I wish that someone had told me these things, not
once, not twice, but continually, because, with the speed
with which life whizzes by, I often forget. So I want to

be your permanent reminder that *you are good enough and that is incredible*. When things get tough, every single moment you feel like you're hanging by a thread with next to no hope left, know you can flick through to the end of this book and, time and time again, read that you're AMAZING.

No, you won't get it right every single time, but who the fuck wants to? Where is the fun in always being right? (Unless you're in an argument and then you're always right.) You can take every single knock, but just remember to laugh at the most inappropriate times. Not only will this sift out the weak people who clearly scare way too easily but it'll mean you have attempted to give yourself a momentary break in what will probably feel like world-ending scenarios. It isn't end-of-world kind of stuff, trust me: until zombies are poking their dicks inside your letterbox and trying to chew your face off, please remember to just take a breath. You can and will get through whatever life is throwing at you.

I have, just like you, wasted so many hours, days, weeks and months on things that actually didn't matter. The size of my clothes, how pretty I looked in those filtered photos and how happy I seemed to everyone around me. Why wasn't I – why weren't you – focusing on that thing inside us that made us happy? And I'm not talking about our G-spot, although that does help. Every breath you take isn't for the happiness of someone else, so take that slow, confident breath for yourself.

You can't please everyone, but who gives a shit if you're happy?? Truly, unless you are shooting heroin into your arms and someone is saying, 'Mate, that isn't a great idea', just know that everyone else can quite frankly get fucked. (I also absolutely do not recommend taking up a drug habit to test this theory.) You will fall in and out of love, friends will come and go, fights will leave you up throughout the night, you will still be tired this time next year, that diet won't go to plan and you will wish you tried harder at it as you hit the beach in that bikini – but remember all the time you have a body you are always going to be ready for that bikini.

I want you to finish reading this book believing you are good enough and you are capable. Four years ago I was the mum of two with a jelly belly who had no direction, who a lot of the time didn't feel much more than someone else's snack bitch, and I felt like 'Maybe this is just my life now??' I'm now the one putting the final words into a book I wrote all by myself, and I'm so proud of myself. And I'm allowed to say that! We are allowed to be proud of ourselves for the things we achieve; we are absolutely entitled to celebrate ourselves once in a while. Don't forget that, and it doesn't need to be the huge stuff. Life is hard, but it's also short, so be sure to make the most of it at every opportunity and don't be ashamed to say no to things you don't want to do. Be brave and be you. I promise that not only is it enough, but that it's all you've got, so make it count.

Thank you for making this weird bitch's dreams come true. I wouldn't be here without you. The love and support is more than you could ever possibly imagine and I will never take it for granted.

Until the next time, my darling, take care, good luck, and remember, above all – learn to love yourself madly, deeply and truly.

Laura X

Acknowledgements

I am at risk of going full-blown Paltrow at the Oscars here and banging on for 12 pages, but I have so many amazing people to thank because without them all this wouldn't be possible. I would like to take this opportunity to thank my incredibly patient, talented and wonderful editor Sara, who has guided me through this whole process, not to mention completely supporting and encouraging my writing ability. I would also like to give thanks to Charlotte, who took her job of helping me edit this book to next level amazing with some of the things she had to Google to understand my lingo, such as: teabagging, along with the whole fantastic team at Ebury who have made this book possible.

I have been blessed with the most supportive family, which is all thanks to my mum and dad; you both are the glue that holds our family together. You have held my hand through some of the hardest moments in my life and loved me at my most unlovable times. I hope one day my children look at me in such admiration as Dave, Emma and I do you. I'd like to give thanks to my brother Dave, who came to the rescue when my laptop broke halfway through writing this book and lent me his ... I promise I'll give it back soon. From the moment I was born, you have all, Lucie and John included, tried your best to look after me. I'll never not be your little sister/baby girl that you feel this overwhelming need to protect and love. Look though guys, I did it! I managed to put my big girl pants on and actually do something to make you proud. Thanks for never giving up on me.

Thank you to my friends, the childhood ones, Lyndsey, Lisa and Vicky, all the way through to the ones I have been fortunate enough to find along the way, Carly, Chara, Jo, Rachaele and Vic. I have been lucky enough to be surrounded by such truly wonderful people who aren't there because they have to be, but instead choose to be there because they want to be, something that will never be lost on me. I am so grateful for all the times you have wiped away my tears, reassured me and told me to believe in myself. I feel very blessed to have such caring people in my life.

I can't let this final moment go by without thanking my amazingly loyal followers on Instagram and Facebook who tune in every day to read my posts and cheer me on. I am always blown away by your love and kindness.

I have been blessed with two of the most amazing children and loving husband who piss me off constantly, and yet there isn't a moment of my life where I'm not thankful to be their mum and wife. Thank you, Steve,

Elliott and Toby, I couldn't be where I am today without you. The unwavering support and love you have shown me, Steve, in my moments of doubt, have meant I have managed to pick myself up, dust myself off and carry on. My three boys, you are my everything, even in the moments where all you're doing is existing because you are, without a doubt, the little specks on this planet that keep me smiling.

I have also dedicated this book to my sister, Emma, who taught me how to be a badass bitch who stands up for what she believes in, and never gives up, even when things feel impossible. You are the best friend I got to grow up with, fight with and look forward to growing old with. Your strength, bravery and guidance have helped me become the positive, confident woman I am today.

Thank you all from the bottom of my heart for helping to make my dreams come true.

X

Fanf**kingtastic F

Tantrums Winging

Bad ass Anxiety St

Depression Love

Marriage Chocolate

Womanhood Bicker

Brain farts Vag ach

Libido loser Honeyn

Supermum Nailing

Takeaways Balls

Skid marks Dry sha

Gin Anti-depressan